The MISSION PRIMER:

Four Steps to an Effective Mission Statement

Richard D. O'Hallaron
David R. O'Hallaron

Mission Incorporated
Richmond, Virginia, USA

The Mission Primer: Four Steps to an Effective Mission Statement

Published by Mission Incorporated
For information address:

Mission Incorporated
2908 Skipton Road
Richmond, VA 23225-1351
Toll Free Phone: (877) 311-4901

ISBN: 0-9676635-0-4

MI 4-11-2000 1st Printing, May 2000

Library of Congress Card Number: 99-091651

Printed in the United States of America

For author information address:

Richard O'Hallaron
Mission Incorporated
2908 Skipton Road
Richmond, VA 23235-1351
phone: (804) 272-4901 &
      (804) 272-4904
fax: (804) 272-1941
email: rdoh@hsc.vcu.edu

David O'Hallaron
School of Computer Science
Carnegie Mellon University
Pittsburgh, PA 15213-3891
phone: (412) 268-8199
fax: (412) 268-5576
email: droh@cs.cmu.edu
www.cs.cmu.edu/~droh

Cover Design: Lisa R. Gray

Contents

About this book

The Mission Primer is a concise guidebook that teaches you how to develop, evaluate, and manage an effective mission statement for your organization.

It is intended for *any* group of people who are organized for *any* purpose. No matter what type or size of organization you belong to, *The Mission Primer* will show you how to develop an effective mission statement for your organization. It works for industrial concerns, non-profits, schools, hospitals, churches, charities, or government agencies; from small three-person sections, to large departments, to giant-multinationals.

The book outlines a simple four-step method for developing effective mission statements. Our unique method is structured, quantifiable, and has a distinct beginning and end. We have used it successfully with dozens of corporate, university, and non-profit clients. The method is based on a set of six laws — what we call *Gast's laws* — that describe the culture of a successful organization. The central idea is that a *good* mission statement describes how the organization intends to comply with Gast's laws.

Although we are sometimes met with initial skepticism from our clients, it never lasts long. Apparently, Gast's laws are based on fundamental and enduring properties of human beings, and thus they resonate strongly with the people who are exposed to them. Gast's laws provide a direction and a clarity that make the process of writing a mission statement focused, time-limited, and rewarding. If you are leading or participating in an effort to develop or evaluate a mission statement for your organization, then you can benefit from the ideas in this book.

Chapter 1

Introduction

A well-crafted mission statement that is used on a daily basis is the hallmark of many great organizations. British Air, Ford Motor, and Johnson & Johnson are shining examples. An effective mission statement is a core document that defines the fundamental objectives of the organization. It is also a cultural contract between the organization and all of its constituents, including employees, suppliers, customers, and owners. When used effectively, it clarifies the long-range goals of the organization, as well as defining how the organization behaves as it strives to reach those goals.

As a leader in an organization, whether a CEO, officer, educator, section head, or shop foreman, you must know how to create, evaluate and manage an effective mission statement. But writing an effective mission statement is hard for most of us. There are many books and articles that talk about the importance of mission statements, but very few that describe how to write an *effective* one. For most of us, the process of writing a mission statement is uncertain, the goals of the process are vague, and the result is often a warm and fuzzy blob that is ignored or ridiculed.

For example, Scott Adams, the creator of the Dilbert comic strip, exploited the uncertainty about writing mission statements in a famous hoax that he perpetrated on some senior executives of Logitech International, the world's largest manufacturer of computer mice. He pulled off the deception with the cooperation of the co-founder and Vice Chairman of the company. An account appeared in the San Jose Mercury News and later in newspapers across the country.

In October, 1997, the Vice Chairman called executives to a meeting

1

with Mr. Adams — alias Ray Mebert — whom they were told was a consultant. The purpose of the meeting was to draft a new mission statement for Logitech's New Ventures Group. Mr. "Mebert" told the group that his credentials included work on Procter and Gamble's *Taste Bright Project*, which he claimed was a secret effort to boost sales by improving the taste of soap.

Executives nodded agreement. Having established his credential as a consultant, Mr. Mebert ridiculed the New Ventures Group's existing mission statement: "The New Ventures Mission is to provide Logitech with profitable growth and related new business areas." He then led an exercise in which managers suggested words and ideas that could eventually be included in a new mission statement. The result of this process was the following mission statement:

> The New Ventures Mission is to scout profitable growth opportunities in relationships, both internally and externally, in emerging, mission inclusive markets, and explore new paradigms and then filter and communicate and evangelize the findings.

Adams's hoax is a funny story that raises a serious question: How could a group of smart people put up with this silliness and accept such a poor mission statement for their organization? It's hard to say for sure, but here is one explanation. The Logitech executives were uncertain about how to go about writing and evaluating mission statements. They probably felt uneasy about the process that Mr. Mebert was putting them through and about the resulting mission statement. But the boss seemed to have a high opinion of the guy, and if they criticized him they might be asked to suggest something better and then justify it. Without a clear understanding of what constitutes a good mission statement, the Logitech execs probably decided that silence was the wiser course.

Hal Lancaster also wrote about the confusion surrounding mission statements in his Wall Street Journal column. At some point, Mr. Lancaster decided to write a personal mission statement. Before undertaking this daunting task, he asked his readers for suggestions. He received over two hundred replies from consultants, coaches, executives, and professionals. In his estimation, these replies made his task more difficult rather than easier because there was so little agreement on what constitutes a good mission statement and how to write one. If people can't agree on how to write a mission statement for a single person, then how are they supposed to write a mission statement for an organization with hundreds or thousands of people?

We've noticed this uncertainty in our management consulting business. Clients routinely complain that they have been working on their mission statement, but are bogged down and need some outside help. For example, a few years ago we were approached by a health care organization in Maryland whose board was having trouble formulating a mission statement. When we investigated, we found that they lacked a conceptual framework around which to build their mission statement, and were bogged down with unresolved objectives about what the organization should be doing. The result was confusion and frustration.

On another occasion we were approached by the CEO of a large health care system in Florida. The health care industry was in the midst of gut-wrenching change, and his organization was attempting to develop a new mission statement that would articulate the strategies they would need to survive. Two previous attempts at developing the mission statement had failed, and again the main culprit was the lack of a coherent framework.

1.1 The method in a nutshell

Our point is that there is a great deal of uncertainty in the business world about what constitutes a good mission statement and how to go about developing one. To clear up the uncertainty, we have developed a simple four-step method for developing effective mission statements. Our method is structured, quantifiable, and has a distinct beginning and end. We have used it successfully with dozens of corporate, university, and non-profit clients, including the organizations in Maryland and Florida mentioned earlier in this chapter that contacted us for help.

Here is the method in a nutshell (also listed in Appendix A):

1. Organize a mission team.

2. Use *Gast's laws* to construct the fundamental objectives of the organization.

3. Use the fundamental objectives to construct the mission statement.

4. Use the mission statement regularly and strategically.

For step 1 we will give you some practical suggestions for organizing a mission team and getting it to work together as a unit. In particular, two techniques called the *value vote* and the *group interview* are especially useful ways to get the process going.

Step 2 introduces the unique and central framework behind our method: a set of six laws (or obligations) that a business must satisfy in order to be successful. These laws were identified by the late Prof. Walter Gast at St. Louis University in the mid 1950s, so we call them *Gast's laws* in his honor. They are listed in Appendix B for your reference.

A mission statement describes the fundamental objectives of a business, and Gast's laws describe the fundamental objectives of a *successful* business.

> *Thus, our method is based on the central idea that a good mission statement describes how an organization intends to comply with Gast's laws.*

Our notion of a mission statement is more inclusive than most. A mission statement should describe the fundamental objectives of the business, and as such includes what people variously refer to as missions, values, values and guiding principles, credos, corporate philosophies, visions, strategic intent, goals, key processes, beliefs, management actions/behaviors, codes of conduct, quality statements, and so on. For example, certain Catholic hospital systems refer to their mission statement as "Our Collective Expression of Mercy, Mission and Shared Values and Beliefs" and "The Philosophy of the Bon Secours Health System". Some Japanese managers refer to their mission as their "Inner Identity". We'll use the term *mission statement* to subsume all of these terms.

Given this definition of a good mission statement, writing a good mission statement is straightforward: Consider each of Gast's laws one at a time, and for each law, decide what the organization should be doing to satisfy that law.

You can also use Gast's laws to evaluate an existing mission statement. For each of the six laws, assign a numbers between 0 and 1 that reflects how well the mission statement address that law. The result is a score, on what we call the *Gast scale*, that measures how well a mission statement addresses Gast's laws, and thus quantifies how good the statement is.

Since our method uses Gast's laws as the framework for both writing and evaluating mission statements, it will only be as useful to you — someone who is leading or participating in the effort to write a mission statement for your organization — as your belief in the truth of the laws. So there is an easy way to evaluate whether or not this book will be helpful to you. If you think Gast's laws describe the culture of a successful organization, then we can provide you with a clear and concise way to develop a good mission statement. If not, then our method won't be helpful to you, and you should look elsewhere for ideas.

We'll describe Gast's laws in more detail in Chapter 2, but since they are the core of the method, we summarize them briefly here. Gast's laws are intriguing and possibly controversial to some because they suggest that making a profit is not the main purpose of a business. Gast's laws say that in order for a business to be successful in the long term, it must not only provide a just return on capital, but it must also do things such as produce a useful commodity or service, increase the wealth of society, provide productive employment opportunities, help employees find meaningful and satisfying work, and pay fair wages. In return, employees (both managers and workers) have an obligation to make the most productive use of their labor and the organization's capital.

Gast's laws are powerful and general because they are based on enduring properties of human beings, and not on the specifics of a particular economic, political, or social environment. For example, people have a deep need for meaningful and rewarding jobs, and Gast claimed that businesses that do better at satisfying that need will be more successful than those that don't.

Because they are based on enduring properties of human beings, Gast's laws resonate strongly with people. The laws have a sense of rightness and justness that people respond to deeply. People often approach the job of developing a mission statement with skepticism and cynicism, yet we have never had a negative experience with any of our clients when we help them develop a mission statement based on Gast's laws.

But you don't have to take just our word for it. It is no accident that the publicly-traded winners of the Malcom Baldrige National Quality Award, which is the most significant award for quality that a U.S. company can receive, have outperformed the Standard & Poors 500 stock index by a 3-to-1 margin since 1994, and also have mission statements that have an extremely high compliance rate with Gast's laws.

Once you have identified a set of fundamental objectives for your organization that satisfy Gast's laws, then you are ready for step 3, which is to use the fundamental objectives from step 2 to construct the actual mission statement. Later in the book, we will give you some practical suggestions for turning the fundamental objectives into an actual mission statement, using mission statements from real companies as examples.

The first three steps help you develop a *good* mission statement, one that describes how the organization intends to address each of Gast's laws. However, in order to turn a good mission statement into an *effective* one, you must use it regularly and strategically in your organization. This is the purpose of step 4. Later in the book we will describe many real-life examples of organizations whose mission statements play a powerful role in the daily and strategic business of the organization.

Our four-step method is effective for a number of reasons:

1. It is simple to understand and implement. Complicated schemes cannot be successfully implemented in most organizations.

2. It has a distinct beginning and an end. People who use our method don't get lost or bogged down in the process of building the mission statement.

3. It produces a mission statement that addresses the needs of all of the constituents of an organization. The resulting mission statement resonates with people, and thus they are more inclined to accept it, promote it, and use it in their daily work lives.

The bottom line is that our method produces mission statements that if well-managed could improve the long-term effectiveness of your organization in many ways, including increased profitability, productivity, return on investment, employee satisfaction, and general prosperity.

1.2   Overview of the rest of the book

This book is meant to be a concise guidebook to help you develop an effective mission statement for your organization, whether it is a small section or department, a regional business, a school, a department in a school, a church, a government agency, a military unit, or a non-profit organization.[1] We've

---

[1] Throughout this book we will use the words *organization* and *business* interchangeably to refer to any group of people organized for some purpose.

used the method outlined in this book successfully with all of these different types of organizations.

In the remainder of the book we'll explain what a mission statement is, how mission statements are used by businesses, and most important, what constitutes a good mission statement. We'll show you how to use Gast's laws to evaluate and modify existing mission statements, how to write new ones from scratch, and how to manage the resulting statements. When you have finished the book, you will have learned a powerful new tool for developing an effective mission statement.

Chapter 2

Gast's Laws

The late Walter Gast was a Professor in the School of Commerce and Finance at St. Louis University during the 1940s and 1950s. In 1958 he joined the faculty of the School of Business at Marquette University, in Milwaukee, WI. He chaired the Marquette MBA program before retiring in the 1960s. While at St. Louis University, Prof. Gast taught a course on Principles of Business Management to Dick O'Hallaron (the first author of this book) during the mid 1950s. He would later become Dick's advisor and mentor.

Prof. Gast opened the first class in his course by saying, "I am going to prove to you that making money is not the main purpose of General Motors." Dick's initial reaction to this was, "This guy is crazy!" However, Prof. Gast was true to his word, and during the next 15 weeks he managed to convince Dick and most of the other students that making money, while extremely important, is not the only purpose of General Motors, or any well-run organization for that matter.

Prof. Gast was neither naive nor a socialist, and he certainly recognized that making money is an essential purpose of a business. However, his point was that for an organization to perform well in the long run, it must recognize that it has other obligations in addition to making a fair rate of return. In particular, Prof. Gast claimed that a business must satisfy the following obligations in order to be most successful:

1. Produce a want-satisfying commodity or service and continually improve the ability to meet needs.

2. Increase the wealth or quality of life of society through the economic use of labor and capital.

3. Provide opportunities for the productive employment of people.

4. Provide opportunities for the satisfaction of normal occupational desires.

5. Provide just wages for labor.

6. Provide a just return on capital.

Prof. Gast never gave these six items a formal name, but we refer to them as *Gast's laws* in his honor. We've listed Gast's laws in Appendix B for easy reference.

You can view Gast's laws in a couple of different lights. On the one hand, they summarize the obligations that a business has to its society (Laws 1-3), to its employees (Laws 4-5), and its owners (Law 6), as well as the obligations that its employees have to the business (Law 2). On the other hand, if we accept that Gast's laws are general attributes of a successful business, then satisfying them should be an objective of that business. In this sense then, Gast's laws can also be viewed as long-term strategic goals of any business or organization. According to Andrew Campbell, Director of the Ashridge Strategic Management Centre in London, England, and one of the foremost authorities on the subject of organizational mission, Gast's Laws are the cornerstone of stakeholder theory. Let's look at them more closely.

Law 1

Law 1: A business must produce a want-satisfying commodity or service, and continually improve its ability to meet needs.

Law 1 says that an organization must have a clear idea of its customers and their needs, and that it must provide a commodity or service to the customers that meets those needs. The organization must also continually improve its ability to recognize and meet the needs of its customers; a business cannot rest on it laurels. Law 1 reminds us that an organization must have a clear idea of its core businesses, and it must always be working to improve its ability to compete in those businesses.

Law 2

Law 2: A business must increase the wealth or quality of life of society through the economic use of labor and capital.

Law 2 addresses the obligation of a business to contribute to the wealth or quality of life of society. In other words, the organization must improve society in general, and the communities where it does business in particular.

By requiring that the organization make productive use of labor and capital as it increases the wealth of society, Law 2 tells us that employees — both workers and managers — have an obligation to ensure that the organization produces high quality goods or services in a cost-effective way. The obligations of employees are a vitally important aspect of Gast's laws. Both the business and its employees have obligations to live up to.

Law 3

Law 3: A business must provide opportunities for the productive employment of people.

Law 3 describes the obligation of a business to society to provide productive employment to people in that society. This is the most controversial and important of Gast's laws because it defines the basic relationship between an organization and its employees, based on respect and trust. (Because of its importance, we will spend a great deal more time discussing this law than the others.)

Law 3 says that a business must have respect for people and that people must be able to trust the organization. A business does not own its employees; employees who join a business do so with intrinsic rights and responsibilities. A business is not obligated to hire people it doesn't need. But if and when it does hire them, it has a responsibility to keep them productively employed. If business is slow, the business should exhaust every means to keep their people productively employed, even when it would be more expedient to simply flush them.

Of course, layoffs are unavoidable in some cases, but Law 3 tells us that because of the respect that it has for all its employees, a business lays off those employees only as a last resort, when absolutely necessary for the survival of the business.

When Prohibition began in the 1920's, Adolphus Busch, the owner of the Anheuser-Busch breweries, had a serious problem. His only product was illegal, and it was not clear what to do with the plant, equipment, and labor designed to produce that product. Perhaps the simplest and most profitable solution in the short-term would have been to just shut down the plants, lay off all the people, and sell the assets.

This was exactly the solution adopted by many other brewers. But Mr. Busch rejected this option, choosing instead to keep his workers employed in other related tasks. Barrel makers made wagons and furniture. The breweries produced bottled water and other non-alcoholic beverages. The grain distribution system was reworked into a new animal feed business.

When Prohibition ended, Anheuser-Busch was light years ahead of the competition, and today they are the leading beer manufacturer in the world. The bottom line is that Mr. Busch felt responsible for his employees and went to enormous lengths to keep them employed, even when it would have been more profitable in the short-term to flush them. Mr. Busch had a good understanding of Law 3!

Malden Mills, in Lawrence, MA, manufactures the wildly popular fabrics known as Polartec and Polarfleece that are used by upscale clothing manufacturers like L.L. Bean, Eddie Bauer, and Patagonia. On December 11, 1995, a catastrophic fire destroyed the textile plant, threatening to put its 3,000 workers out of work. Instead, the owner of the firm, Aaron Feuerstein, did a remarkable thing. He kept the employees on the payroll for three months, at a cost of millions of dollars, while he rebuilt the plant.

When asked why he made such a remarkable gesture in an interview for Parade magazine, he explained that he considers his workers an asset rather than an expense. Further, he believes that his job goes beyond making money for the shareholders. Says Mr. Feuerstein, "I have an equal responsibility to the community. It would have been unconscionable to put 3,000 people on the streets and deliver a death blow to the city of Lawrence."

Mr. Feuerstein not only understands the responsibility that his business has to his community, he also has built a business with a deep respect for its employees. With respect to layoffs, Mr. Feuerstein says, "That goes straight against the American Dream. You work hard and should make a good living and have a good retirement. I could get rid of the workers who earn $15 an hour and bring in a contract house that will pay $7 an hour. But that breaks the spirit and trust of the employees. If you close a factory because you can get work done for $2 an hour elsewhere, then you break the American Dream."

Both the responsibility that he feels toward his community and the respect that he has for his employees are based on good business sense. Says Mr. Feuerstein, "The quality of our product is paramount, and it's the employee who makes the quality. If quality slips, the employee is in a position to destroy your profit."

His loyalty has been repaid in higher productivity. "Before the fire, that plant produced 130,000 yards a week. A few weeks after the fire, it was up to 230,000 yards. Our people became very creative. They were willing to work 25 hours a day."

Mr. Feuerstein has probably never heard of Gast's laws, but he intuitively understands all of them, in particular the respect for people that is central to Law 3.

It is reasonable to wonder if Law 3 (which was conceived 50 years ago) is still valid today. The business environment is certainly much different now than it was then. Competition is fierce and conducted on a global scale. Organizations are subject to mergers and acquisitions at a dizzying rate. Jobs are being outsourced to foreign countries. However, we claim that none of these phenomena are really new. Although the rate and magnitude of the changes is different, the fundamental responsibilities of a business have not changed. Thus, Gast's Laws in general, and Law 3 in particular, are more important than ever.

Here are three examples of business executives, each with a good intuitive understanding of Law 3, who were recently involved in mergers and acquisitions. Two of them (Crutsinger and Goodwin) were involved in the sales of large companies. The third executive (Renz) has acquired a number of companies.

Bob Crutsinger, the former President and Vice Chairman of Wetterau

Incorporated, St. Louis, MO, described his experience with a merger in 1992 between Wetterau and Supervalue, of Minneapolis, MN. Wetterau had been in business since 1869, did an estimated 6.4 billion dollars a year in business, and had operations in 34 states throughout the U.S.

In a recent interview we asked Crutsinger about Wetterau's mission, how influential it was within the organization, and what impact it had on the merger strategy. Here is his reply:

> Wetterau had an excellent mission statement called the *Wetterau Creed*, developed by Ted Wetterau. It was very influential in shaping their strategic plans, making policy and business decisions. It was well known, understood and for the most part well appreciated by management and 16,000 employees. As a matter of fact it was not unusual for an employee from a store, or a truck driver in the field to make an appointment with Mr. Wetterau or myself to discuss some policy or action the individual thought might be in conflict with the Wetterau mission. When it was deemed that the employee was right, remedial action was taken.
>
> The mission created a culture throughout the organization that the employees liked. Management worked very hard to preserve this culture. One example of our efforts was our Christmas travel. We spent several weeks each Christmas traveling throughout our company locations just to meet with employees on the job, shake hands with them, wish them and their families a Merry Christmas, and get to know them better. Ted Wetterau and I worked at this, and we knew many of our employees by their first and last name. It was important to us and to the employees. After the company was sold, one of the things the employees missed the most was the previous culture of the organization. We were a close family.

It sounds great, but if Wetterau thought so highly of their employees, then why did they sell the business?

> We had to look at what we visioned the grocery business to look like in the new millennium. We could see that Wetterau had to grow considerably to meet the competition, and stay healthy

in most of the areas we already served. That would take a great deal of capital. We didn't have the ability to raise that capital, so the next best thing was to merge with a company that fit with our organization. Supervalue fit that profile. If we had not done this, our employees would have suffered greatly, after the turn of the century. Many people would have lost their jobs. Not only that, many of our employees were heavily invested in the company through stock options, and they would have lost accumulated savings in that respect.

Did the mission of Wetterau have any impact on the sale condition; did Wetterau do anything to protect the employees?

Yes we did. From the very beginning we had our employees in mind. Wetterau had for many years a stock option program for employees. This program would vest on a graduating scale after 5–10 years of employment. Our goal was to reward long-term employees with options, and to encourage our people to stay with us. The program worked and was well received.

The problem was that with the sale many employees were caught in between vesting anniversaries. So we insisted that on the day of the sale, all employees were vested, regardless of where they were in the time warp. We also knew that some of our people, especially at the headquarters level were going to be redundant. We did everything to help them find other jobs (with Supervalue or elsewhere), provided outplacement services, gave special separation bonuses and did everything we could to soften the blow.

Our feeling was that everyone was important, each person involved had helped make Wetterau successful, and we did not want to leave the company without doing our best to work with all concerned to make the merger as fair as possible. I think we succeeded in this effort.

Did Supervalue have the same interest in the Wetterau employees?

Supervalue did not have the personal attachment we had to our fellow employees, but they recognized that it was our employees who made Wetterau such a success. They valued our employees.

William H. Goodwin Jr., who heads up CCA Industries Inc. in Richmond, VA, is an example of an another executive who was concerned about his employees when they were involved in a company sale. Goodwin sold his company, AMF, for over a billion dollars in 1996. When the sale was completed, he took 50 million dollars of his proceeds, and distributed it among the employees. Here is his account:

> I felt a responsibility for the sale, and for the people who built the business. Everybody got a bonus of approximately 2 months salary. Some got more. The idea was to give a bonus, so that in those cases where people were not able to stay with the new company, this would help give a kick to their severance packages. We also negotiated a severance pay package for any employee who was laid off within the first two years after the sale. This gave the new company and employees a chance to get used to each other, yet made it a bit painful to terminate within two years.
>
> I did this for a couple of reasons. First of all, I made so much money on this sale, I could never spend it all. Secondly, I felt a responsibility to share the profit with those who had built up the company in the first place. Thirdly, it was tax deductible. I also gave a bonus to a half a dozen or more people who were not with the business for one reason or another, but who had contributed substantially to it before they left. I called one person in England to tell him I was writing him a check for $100,000. Another person received $50,000. Both of these people worked for AMF and at one time did a lot for the company, but for one reason or another left the company. Some of those who received a bonus were former directors, or consultants who were a great help. One of our past officers received three million dollars.

Do all businesses have this responsibility to their employees and constituents?

> The buyer doesn't feel the responsibility to employees of the company bought. The seller, on the other hand, has worked with

the people involved and does have a responsibility, and should feel this. In my opinion, a seller has the obligation to negotiate for the employees of the company being sold, especially for those one knows will be out of a job, or will be terminated within the next two years. You must take care of those you know who will be displaced, and then make it painful to terminate within two years. This keeps everyone honest.

I hope your story is going to address the responsibilities of the employees to the company. Even though the company has a lot more power than the employee, it is still a two way street, and many executives are disheartened by the shoddy way some employees treat the company. Let me give some examples. I am on the board of one of our large universities in Virginia. We recently had one of our key employees, abruptly leave a $200,000 plus job dealing with the Y2K problem. The individual left right in the middle of a crisis. Another example involved a young lady with a very good job with one of the large consulting firms. She became pregnant with twins, and because of this was given a three month early paid leave of absence. On top of that she got the usual three months paid leave. After she took six months of paid leave, she then told the company she would not return to work. Is that fair?

Any regrets?

Only one. I wish I had given twice the amount, especially to the lower paid people. I kept track of all the notes I received after the distribution of the bonuses. I still have them. I hope some day to sit down and read them all again, before I meet the Good Lord. The nicest notes seemed to come from the lowest paid people. Some were written in pencil, and they could hardly be read, but they were beautiful. I wish I had done more, especially for the lower paid people.

Daniel J. Renz, President and CEO of Summit Marketing Group Inc. in St. Louis, MO, mirrors Gast's views on Law 3 with respect to the touchy issue of layoffs. He believes that business executives are not being held accountable regarding the issue of large layoffs. Many of them announce big cuts, and then are rewarded like heroes for biting the bullet. For the most part, however, the problem is that undisciplined management allowed the companies to become bloated in the first place. This management practice is an injustice to the employees who must pay the price.

Renz believes, as does Gast, that business executives have an obligation to see to it that no more employees are hired as full-time permanent employees than will be needed long term. First, he does not subscribe to lifetime employment philosophies, but feels that when an employee is hired he or she has a reasonable opportunity to stable employment. Secondly, he believes top management must manage in such a way as to find other alternatives to layoffs during adversity. He gave an example of one of the companies owned by his group that lost 30% of its business, due to outside mergers involving some of their key customers. Rather than lay off a substantial number of the people effected, he worked with the division managers to find ways to regrow the business so these people did not have to be laid off. The division was given six months to work things out. By the end of the six month period, the division had not only recouped an original amount of business lost, but had exceeded by 15% the volume of the original business.

According to Renz, whose organization has been involved in 8 acquisitions within the last few years:

> We spend from 6-18 months in discussions with a company before acquiring it. This is a long time when considering industry averages. Our purposes, however, are to get to know the people we are considering acquiring, and make sure they will fit our management profile. We are also up front with them about how our method of operation will effect the people involved. We will identify ahead of time those who may have to be laid off.

> Our philosophy is to provide these people with every resource we have to help them find other suitable employment. We research the local practices for severance packages and try to do one and half to two times the standard.

> We are very aggressive in our efforts to keep the full time permanent employment to an optimum size. We have had times when we would bring in temporary people to cover for a year or so. However, we made it clear the jobs involved were temporary,

but did give them an opportunity to apply for a permanent job if one became available during the temporary period.

Layoffs are not a statistical matter. When laying off people you are dealing with human beings who depend on the job in question. They have goals of their own, and in many cases a spouse and family depending on that job also. A person's job is one of the most important things in a person's life. It has to be treated as such.

Law 4

Law 4: A business must provide opportunities for the satisfaction of normal occupational desires.

Law 4, like Law 3, is based on the crucial values of respect and trust. This law is based on the premise that people take their jobs seriously. They are not intrinsically lazy and trying to get by with the least possible effort. Their jobs and careers are important. They have a strong desire to make them as useful and fulfilling as possible. People naturally dream of meaningful work, just compensation, leadership, recognition, training, fairness, challenges, security, acceptance by their peers, physical safety, opportunities for creativity, advancement, and a sense of participation in the conditions and rewards of the business. Law 4 reminds us of the responsibility of each business to try to provide opportunities for employees to satisfy these normal occupational desires. We think of satisfying Law 4 as striving to provide a great quality of work life for the employees, an environment where people look forward to coming to work every day.

Law 5

Law 5: A business must provide just wages for labor.

The need for just compensation is so important that it is addressed separately by Law 5. Depending on the particular business, this can include compensation for labor performed by employees (including workers and managers), and subcontractors, or products or services supplied by vendors. Of course, what constitutes fair compensation is a very difficult question. The essence of Law 5 is that a business recognizes the importance of compensating its employees, subcontractors, and vendors fairly, and works diligently toward that end.

Bobby Ukrop, one of the owners of Ukrop's Super Markets in Richmond, VA, tells an interesting story about the importance of valuing vendors and treating them fairly. Ukrop's is a regional grocery chain with a national reputation for being well-managed. It has been written up in Fortune and Time magazines. On January 12, 2000, Ukrop's made Fortune magazine's listing of the 100 best companies to work for.

When Bobby was a young boy, he and his father went to the wholesale market one morning to buy vegetables for their stores. They bought a load of potatoes from the potato vendor at a certain price early in their shopping expedition. Later in the morning they realized they needed another load of potatoes. When they returned to the potato vendor's stall, he was just getting ready to leave and had sharply reduced the prices for his potatoes. To the son's surprise, the father paid the original price for the extra load of potatoes rather than the reduced price. When the son asked why, the father explained that it was his mistake in not knowing how many loads of potatoes he needed, and the vendor shouldn't have to pay the price for the father's mistake. He had a long-term relationship with the vendor, and by paying the original price, helped create trust and loyalty in the vendor that would more than offset the expense of paying full price for the second load of potatoes.

Law 6

Law 6: A business must provide a just return on capital.

Finally, Law 6 refers to the obligation that an organization has to provide a just (reasonable) return to the people who invest in or contribute to the organization. By a just return, Gast means that a business should attempt to maximize its profits, subject to the constraints imposed by the other five laws. For example, a business shouldn't attempt to maximize profits by paying slave wages to its employees or by laying off employees unnecessarily.

For a private business, Law 6 identifies the obligation of the business to stockholders or owners who expect their investment to increase in value. For an educational institution, the obligation is to its financial supporters, families, students, and outside organizations who pay tuition, and to its research sponsors. For a government agency, this obligation is to the taxpayers who are paying the bills. For the non-profit charitable organization, the obligation is to the sponsors, the contributors, and the community served. In each case, those who contribute capital to the business expect it to be used wisely and productively.

Many people incorrectly assume that turning a profit is the only purpose of a business. Gast's essential insight is that while profit is obviously important, it is not the only purpose of a business. Other obligations, embodied in the other five laws, are equally important.

□□□

Gast's laws are natural laws in the sense that they are based on fundamental and unchanging properties of human beings, and not on any particular economic or political system. They are based on basic values of trust, respect for people, and quality that resonate strongly and naturally with all of us. Thus they apply to any type of organization, including private businesses, non-profit businesses, churches, schools, and government agencies. The laws also apply to smaller groups of people within these larger entities.

The premise of this book is that Gast's laws describe the objectives of a successful organization. Even in very competitive environments, businesses that adhere to Gast's laws will tend to perform better than those that don't. To a hard-nosed executive struggling in a downsized firm to make aggressive quarterly goals, Gast's laws might seem overly idealistic and naive. However, the laws can be directly tied to financial performance.

In 1987 the Congress of the United States created the Malcom Baldrige National Quality Award to recognize U.S. companies that significantly improved the quality of their products. The Commerce Department was assigned to manage the competition for the awards, which are given out annually to up to six companies. Since 1988, 31 different companies have won the award. One company, Solectron, has won the award twice. Appendix C gives the complete list of winners.

The Commerce Department's research arm, the National Institute of Standards and Technology (NIST), formerly known as the National Bureau of Standards, studies the performance of the Baldrige Award winners in order to help justify the value of the awards (and indirectly the value of the government agency that administers the awards). In a stock investment study performed in February, 1997, NIST determined that the publicly-traded winners of the Baldrige Award have outperformed the Standard & Poors 500 stock index by a 3-to-1 margin since 1988. Interestingly, organizations that made it to the final site-visit stage of the competition, but did not win the award, still outperformed the Standard & Poors 500 by a 2-1 margin.

Clearly, the Baldrige Award winners are high-performing organizations, and if Gast is right, then we would expect the mission statements of these high performing organizations to address all six of his laws. So we set about trying to obtain the mission statements from as many Baldrige Award winners as possible. Ultimately we were able to obtain copies of mission statements from 12 of the 21 winners in the period 1988 — 1994, and we checked them for compliance with Gast's laws. We assigned each mission statement a maximum of six points, one for each law. For each law, if the mission statement indicated that the corporation was trying to adhere to that law, then we assigned 1 point, otherwise we assigned 0 points.

The results were quite interesting. The Baldrige Award winners scored 67 out of a possible 72 points, which is a compliance rate of 93%. So Baldrige Award winners, which outperform the Standard & Poors 500 stock index by a factor of 3-1, also have a very high compliance rate with Gast's laws. The point we want to drive home is that Gast's laws are not simply idealistic, naive, and wishful thinking. Rather, they reflect the cultures of some of the best performing businesses in the U.S.

Of course, Prof. Gast was not the only person to recognize that a business has obligations besides achieving a just rate of return for its owners. Other great business leaders have had similar insights. For example, Donald Peterson of Ford Motor Company led a revolution in the culture of the American automobile industry that helped save the industry. The mission statement that Mr. Peterson crafted for Ford recognizes that while profit is important, it represents a measure, not the purpose, of the organization. Mr. Peterson says, "Profits are the ultimate measure of how efficiently we provide customers with the best products for their needs." The differences are very subtle, but they have helped to substantially change the culture of the Ford Motor Company and turn around it's financial performance. In fact, Mr. Peterson claims that the day that the Board of Directors adopted the new mission statement marked the beginning of the turnaround for Ford.

As another example, Konosuke Matsushita, the late founder of the huge Matsushita Corporation, had a surprisingly similar view of profits. "Profit is a yardstick with which to measure the degree of social contribution made by an enterprise. Thus, profit is a result rather than a goal."

When Gast introduced his laws, many were skeptical. Many highly successful companies didn't seem to care about customers, employees, or the community. The major emphasis of these companies was to make money. People were a means to this end, and products and services were produced on pretty much a take it or leave it basis.

We knew that companies in industries such as the automotive industry, the steel industry, some unions, and the railroad industry had little regard for the principles behind Gast's laws, and yet they seemed to be successful. What we have come to believe since then is that although these companies were successful at one time, they ultimately failed (or almost failed in the case of the automotive industry) because they didn't understand the business they were in, and were concerned primarily with short term success, which they measured for the most part by the bottom line. They ignored Gast's laws and ultimately paid the price.

Of course, business management is not a science, and there is no way to either prove or disprove the validity of Gast's laws in a scientific sense. However, 40 years of running large organizations and consulting with other organizations have convinced us that Gast's laws represent a clear and sound guide for running a successful business. As such, they constitute the crucial framework for developing a mission statement that has impact on the daily life of your organization.

Chapter 3

Model Mission Statements

A mission statement identifies the fundamental objectives of a business.

By *fundamental objectives* we mean a set of high-level goals that are neither time-specific nor quantified. For example, "providing low-cost high-quality rental cars to business travelers" might be an appropriate fundamental objective for a company like Avis. On the other hand, "providing business travelers with GM cars at less than $25 per day" is not appropriate because it is too quantified. Similarly, "providing a reasonable return for our stockholders" is appropriate, while "achieving annual revenues of $100M within the next two years" is not appropriate because it is time-specific and quantified. These types of specific quantified goals are more appropriate for a traditional strategic plan, not a mission statement.

Companies use mission statements in a variety of ways, some more effectively than others. Some companies create a mission statement, frame it, hang it on the wall, and then never refer to it again, except maybe in the annual report. Other companies might use the mission statement sporadically to help attract new business, to recruit employees, or to enhance the image of the company. Clearly, these companies don't get much benefit from their mission statements.

Not everyone is sold on the value of mission statements. One of our graduate students, a practicing physician and chairman of his group practice, once told the class, "We don't have a written mission statement. We know what we are about." This may be true, but if you've ever tried to write about some idea you have, then you quickly learn that the process of putting ideas down on paper exposes gaps and fuzziness in your thinking.

Other businesses use their mission statement more effectively, as a tool to guide the organization's strategic planning effort, to help set day-to-day priorities, to evaluate new or ongoing programs, and to evaluate the policies and practices of the organization.

Appendices D through J contain examples of model mission statements that are *good* in the sense that they address Gast's laws, and *effective* in the sense that they play a powerful role in the daily life of their organization. Some of the model mission statements were developed by our clients using the method described in this book (a unit of Anheuser-Busch, the Virginia Commonwealth University/Medical College of Virginia School of Allied Health Professions, and the Virginia Commonwealth University Department of Psychology). Others were developed independently by outstanding companies who weren't aware of Gast's laws, but produced excellent mission statements nonetheless (British Airways, Ford Motor, Johnson & Johnson, and Ukrop's Super Markets).

The Anheuser-Busch Technology Acquisition Team is a section within Anheuser-Busch that negotiates contracts for computer and communications equipment and hires data processing consultants for the company. This is a good example of a mission statement written for a group within a large organization. It has been in daily use since 1994.

Sir Colin Marshall, Chairman of the Board, arrived at British Airways in 1983. In 1986 he and his colleagues developed British Airways' first formal mission statement. In the ensuing years he and his colleagues turned the airline around and transformed it into one of the top-rated airlines in the world. Mr. Marshall shared with us the following insights about the role of the mission statement at British Airways:

> Our own *Mission and Goals* forms a credo that commits us to standards of excellence in the way we conduct our business, the way we serve our customers, and the way in which we play our part in the community at large. We also believe firmly that excellence in the way we serve and support each other within British Airways is the only true way of building long-lasting integrity into our products and services. In other words, we can only expect the customer to believe in us if we believe in ourselves. Our *Mission and Goals* are our railroad tracks to success.

Donald Peterson, the visionary who revolutionized the culture of the American automobile industry, shared with us the following insight on Ford Motor Company's mission statement:

> Our mission statement represents the foundation of how we conduct our daily business. Furthermore, it has provided since the early 1980's the cornerstone for our present success, and importantly, guided our understanding that continuous improvement is a necessity for continuing prosperity in the future.

When Mr. Peterson took over as Ford's president and chief operating officer in 1980, Ford was going through difficult times. Says Mr. Peterson, "In 1980 alone we lost more than $1.5 billion, then the second highest one-year loss in U.S. corporate history. To make matters worse, our market share was slipping steadily, and customers were increasingly disenchanted with our cars."

By the time he retired in 1990, Mr. Peterson had turned the company around, and Ford Motor Company was profitable and healthy. Shortly after his retirement was announced, Mr. Peterson was asked if he could identify a moment that marked Ford's turnaround. He said, "Ford's comeback stems from a management meeting in 1984 when the company's leadership adopted the *Company Mission, Values, and Guiding Principles.*"

The oldest and perhaps most famous mission statement is the elegant Johnson & Johnson Credo, which was first written in 1943 by the company founder Robert Wood Johnson. As early as 1935, in a pamphlet entitled "Try Reality", Mr. Johnson was advocating a view similar to Mr. Gast's that emphasized a corporation's responsibilities to customers, employees, community, and stockholders. Eight years later, Mr. Johnson published these ideas as a one page *Credo*, which he sold throughout the corporation, urging his management to apply it as part of their everyday business philosophy. By discussing customers first and stockholders last, the Credo reflects Mr. Johnson's practical minded view that the business and stockholders were best served by putting the customer first.

While the Johnson & Johnson Credo has been updated over the years to recognize concern for the earth's environment and the balance between work and family life, the spirit of the document remains unchanged, and in the words of a Johnson & Johnson spokesperson,

... Its principles have become a constant goal, as well as a source of inspiration, for all who are part of the Johnson & Johnson family of companies. About fifty years after it was first introduced, the Credo continues to guide the destiny of the world's largest and most diversified health care company.

The same spokesperson credits the Credo with helping to successfully guide the company through the Tylenol crises of 1982 and 1986, when the company's product was adulterated with cyanide by a criminal and turned into a murder weapon. "With the future of the company at stake, Johnson & Johnson managers and employees made countless decisions that were inspired by the philosophy embodied in the Credo."

Smaller regional organizations also take their mission statements to heart and use them effectively. Ukrop's Super Markets — the number one grocery chain in central Virginia, with over 24 stores — has an excellent mission statement that was written with input from hundreds of employees (or associates in the Ukrop's terminology) throughout the company. According to a company spokesperson, the **Ukrop's** mission statement is an important part of the daily work life:

The widespread participation of associates in this process has strengthened their commitment to and alignment with our vision, mission, and shared values. We have encouraged our associates to memorize and recite the vision, mission and shared values of our company. After doing so, they receive a "Shared Values" pin, and their name is listed on the "Shared Values Honor Roll" in their store. During the 1994 fiscal year, more than 2,600 of our 5,000 associates recited their shared values.

Schools and departments can also benefit from mission statements. The Virginia Commonwealth University Department of Psychology in Richmond, Virginia, one of our clients, developed an excellent mission statement as part of a restructuring of the Department in the mid 1990's.

The Virginia Commonwealth University/Medical College of Virginia School of Allied Health Professions is another one of our clients who developed a new mission statement in the mid 1990's.

We'll refer to these model mission statements throughout the rest of the book.

Chapter 4

What is a Good Mission Statement?

We've seen in the previous chapter that a good mission statement can be an effective tool that powerfully affects the success of an organization. But what in the world is a *good* mission statement?

A mission statement is a document that describes the fundamental objectives of a business. Since Gast's laws capture the fundamental objectives of a *successful* business, *a good mission statement consists of a set of fundamental objectives that describe how an organization intends to comply with Gast's laws.*

We measure the quality of a mission statement using a tool called the *Gast scale*. For each law, we assign a number between 0 and 1, for a maximum total score of 6. For a given law, if the mission statement doesn't address the law, then it gets a 0 for that law. If the mission statement addresses the law perfectly, then the score for that law is 1. If the statement partially addresses the law, then we assign a partial score between 0 and 1. The sum of the scores is our estimate of the quality of the mission statement on the Gast scale. Each law receives an equal weight in our scoring scheme because we feel that all of the objectives are equally important.

For example, Mr. Mebert's mission statement for the Logitech New Ventures Group receives a 1 out of 6 on the Gast scale because it only addresses Law 1. This quantifies our initial qualitative sense that it wasn't any good.

As another example, let's look at how we might use the Gast scale to evaluate and improve a real mission statement culled from the annual report of a major bank that we'll refer to as *GoodBank*.

> GoodBank's mission is to provide the maximum economic return to our shareholders over the long term, and to contribute to the economic vitality and quality of life of our communities.
>
> We believe this is accomplished by providing an environment that encourages the individual potential of our employees and emphasizes the highest quality services for our customers.

Is this a good mission statement? On the Gast scale, it receives 3.3 (out of 6) points, so there would appear to be room for improvement. Let's look in detail at how we arrived at this score. For each law, we will discuss how well the statement addresses that law, assign a score, and then modify the statement so that it does a better job of addressing the law. The modifications are shown in boldface type.

Law 1

There are a number of problems in this mission statement with respect to Law 1. First, the statement is unclear about the core business (or businesses) of the bank. Second, the statement could be more specific about the nature of the bank's customers. Third, the statement doesn't address the need for continual improvement of its services. Finally, the key notion of providing a service to customers is buried in the second paragraph, almost as an afterthought. *Score: 0.5.*

Here is the revised version that does a better job of addressing Law 1. We've revised the statement to be more specific about the core business, the customers, and the need for continuous improvement, and we have given first-class status to the objective of providing service to customers.

> Goodbank's mission is to provide **the highest quality financial services for the individuals, businesses, and financial institutions that we serve**, to provide the maximum economic return to our shareholders over the long term, and to contribute to the economic vitality and quality of life of our communities.
>
> We believe this is accomplished by providing an environment that encourages the individual potential of our employees

and that continuously improves our ability to serve our customers.

Law 2

The statement recognizes the bank's obligation to increase the economic vitality and quality of life in the community. However, it fails to recognize the obligation of the employees, including managers and workers, to be productive and efficient. *Score: 0.5.*

Here is the revised version that addresses the need for employees to be efficient so that the bank can provide cost-efficient services.

> Goodbank's mission is to provide the highest quality financial services **at a reasonable cost to** the individuals, businesses, and financial institutions that we serve, to provide the maximum economic return to our shareholders over the long term, and to contribute to the economic vitality and quality of life of our communities.
>
> We believe this is accomplished by providing an environment that encourages the individual potential of our employees and that continuously improves our ability to serve our customers.

Law 3

The GoodBank mission statement is on the right track with its encouragement of individual potential. However, it doesn't speak directly to the importance of the people in the organization. *Score: 0.9.*

Here is the revised version for Law 3, with an explicit reference to the importance of the people that contribute to the bank's mission.

> Goodbank's mission is to provide the highest quality financial services at a reasonable cost to the individuals, businesses, and financial institutions that we serve, to provide the maximum economic return to our shareholders over the long term, and to

contribute to the economic vitality and quality of life of our communities.

We believe this is accomplished by providing an environment **that recognizes the people of GoodBank as our greatest asset**, that encourages the individual potential of our employees, and that continuously improves our ability to serve our customers.

Law 4

With its emphasis on encouraging individual potential, the GoodBank mission statement does a good job of addressing Law 4. However, a minor criticism is that the statement could be even more aggressive by recognizing GoodBank's obligation to help employees *maximize* their potential. *Score: 0.9*.

Here is the revised version for Law 4:

> Goodbank's mission is to provide the highest quality financial services at a reasonable cost to the individuals, businesses, and financial institutions that we serve, to provide the maximum economic return to our shareholders over the long term, and to contribute to the economic vitality and quality of life of our communities.
>
> We believe this is accomplished by providing an environment that recognizes the people of GoodBank as our greatest asset, that **maximizes** the individual potential of our employees, and that continuously improves our ability to serve our customers.

Law 5

The subject of compensation for employees, vendors, and contractors is ignored in GoodBank's mission statement. *Score: 0.0.*

Here is a revised version for Law 5:

Goodbank's mission is to provide the highest quality financial services at a reasonable cost to the individuals, businesses, and financial institutions that we serve, to provide the maximum economic return to our shareholders over the long term, and to contribute to the economic vitality and quality of life of our communities.

We believe this is accomplished by providing an environment that recognizes the people of GoodBank as our greatest asset, that maximizes the individual potential of our employees, that continuously improves our ability to serve our customers, **and that provides fair compensation to our employees, vendors, and subcontractors.**

Law 6

By focusing on maximum return for share holders, the statement could be perceived as diminishing the organization's obligations to its other constituents, such as employees, contractors, suppliers, and the community. *Score: 0.5.*

Here is the revised statement, modified to better satisfy the spirit of Law 6. We use the phrase "reasonable economic return" rather than "maximum economic return" to give the impression that while profits are a serious and important obligation, they are not the only obligation.

Goodbank's mission is to provide the highest quality financial services at a reasonable cost to the individuals, businesses, and financial institutions that we serve, to provide a **reasonable** economic return to our shareholders over the long term, and to contribute to the economic vitality and quality of life of our communities.

We believe this is accomplished by providing an environment that recognizes the people of GoodBank as our greatest asset, that maximizes the individual potential of our employees, that continuously improves our ability to serve our customers, and that provides fair compensation to our employees, vendors, and subcontractors.

The final version of the GoodBank mission statement now receives a perfect score of 6.0 on the Gast scale. By this measure at any rate, it is significantly better than the original mission statement.

□□□

It is important to realize that a mission statement with a perfect score on the Gast scale is not necessarily a perfect mission statement that can't be improved. The Gast scale is a helpful tool that measures compliance with Gast's laws; it says nothing about the beauty of the language used in the mission statement or about its ability to inspire people.

The real value of the Gast scale is that it provides us, for the first time, with a quantifiable measure of how well a mission statement adheres to fundamental objectives that are common to successful organizations.

So how do our model mission statements in the appendices stack up on the Gast scale? Here is a summary of the scores.

Organization/Law	1	2	3	4	5	6	Total
AB Tech. Acq. Team	1	1	1	1	1	1	6
British Airways	0.5	1	1	1	1	1	5.5
Ford Motor	1	1	1	1	0	1	5
Johnson & Johnson	1	1	1	1	1	1	6
Ukrop's	1	1	1	1	1	1	6
VCU Dept. of Psych.	1	1	1	1	1	1	6
VCU/MCV School of AHP	1	1	1	1	1	1	6

According to our interpretation of the Gast scale, all of the mission statements in the appendices are pretty good.

The British Airways statement, with a score of 5.5, is appealing because it is concise and elegant. Its only flaw is that it fails to address the importance of continually improving its ability to engage in its core businesses.

Ford Motor, with a score of 5, loses a point because it fails to address the issue of compensation (Law 5). But it is otherwise an excellent statement and has had a tremendous impact worldwide.

The other statements all receive perfect scores. Of these, the Johnson & Johnson mission statement is perhaps the most remarkable because it was written so long ago, and yet, with only minor additions, is still fresh and current today. It remains an integral part of the life at the Johnson & Johnson. The longevity and usefulness of this document is one of the key factors that convinced us of the generality and truth of Gast's laws. In the chapters to follow, we will outline a method for using Gast's laws to develop mission statements.

Chapter 5

Four Steps to an Effective Mission Statement

We have developed a step-by-step method that uses Gast's laws as a framework for developing mission statements. We have used this method successfully with dozens of our clients. It works because it provides people with a clear structure and a set of specific tasks that keep them from getting bogged down in the sort of endless circular arguments that often arise when people try to resolve difficult strategic issues. This chapter gives an overview of our method. Chapters 6 through 9 will elaborate.

Our method consists of four steps:

1. Organize a mission team.

2. Use Gast's laws to construct the fundamental objectives of the organization.

3. Use the fundamental objectives to construct the mission statement.

4. Use the mission statement regularly and strategically.

For the first step, organize a cross-section of the people in your organization whose job is to develop the mission statement. This group is called the *mission team*. For the second step, the mission team considers Gast's laws one by one. For each law, make a list of the fundamental objectives that are necessary to help the organization satisfy the obligations described by that law. These objectives form the raw material that a subset of the mission team will eventually craft into a mission statement in step 3. If you follow these first three steps, you will have developed a *good* mission statement. But it will only be an *effective* mission statement if it is used regularly and strategically by the rest of your organization, which is the purpose of the fourth step.

The next four chapters describe our method in more detail.

Chapter 6

Organize a Mission Team

A mission statement can be effective only if there is consensus that it truly reflects the objectives of both the people in the organization and the stakeholders affected by it. We can't overemphasize the importance of achieving this consensus. A mission statement must speak not only to the employees, but also to the vendors, stockholders, customers, and, in general, all of the constituents of that business. These people must believe that they will benefit from the mission statement.

In our experience, the best way to get this consensus is for the leader of the organization to charge a representative cross section of people, called the *mission team*, with the task of developing the mission statement. Each member of the team should have an equal vote.

This group approach has several advantages. By including a cross section of people in the organization, you increase the chances of coming up with a set of objectives that truly reflect the organization. The resulting mission statement is also easier to sell to the rest of the organization because the members of the mission team have already bought in, and thus can sell it effectively to their co-workers.

For example, over 80 people were involved in some phase of writing or reviewing the mission statement for the School of Allied Health Professions. With so many people actively involved, we avoided the sense that the mission statement was being imposed from above, and the final document was accepted and internalized by the members of the school.

As another example, a Navy medical service corps that we worked with sent a draft of the mission statement to over 900 members of the medical service corps, asking for their comments before making the final revisions.

On the other hand, we were once asked to review the mission statement of a division of General Electric, to see why people didn't seem to like it. Two weeks after it was issued, it was difficult to find a copy for us to review; apparently most people had just thrown it in the wastebasket. No one knew who had worked on the statement. The mission statement was prepared without any contribution by those it affected, was not sold to the rest of the organization, and thus had no impact.

There are a couple of important principles to keep in mind when forming a mission team. First, the head of the organization must lead the effort and must be willing to make a long-term commitment to its success. Second, the leader must choose people for the mission team who are upbeat, positive, and who really want to see the team succeed.

We have been asked a number of times to help revive a failed mission effort. In most cases they failed because they had the wrong people on their mission team, people who were not committed to its success. On the other hand, we have found that mission teams composed of the right people invariably succeed.

While we prefer the group approach, we should point out that excellent mission statements can and have been developed in isolation by individuals and then sold successfully throughout the business. For example, the excellent Johnson & Johnson mission statement was developed by the CEO and then later accepted and internalized by the organization.

6.1   The value vote

When we work with mission teams in our consulting practice, the first thing we do with the team is to hold a *value vote*. A value vote is a technique that helps a mission team articulate the values that the team would like to see in the culture of the organization. A series of votes results in a small list of values. These can be values that are already part of the culture, or they can be new values that the team would like to see become part of the culture.

We have found the value vote to be enormously helpful for a number of reasons. The process of reaching a consensus on the shared values of the organization helps to unify the team and give it a sense of unity of purpose. But more important, the small set of shared values that the team identifies helps the group to reach consensus later on when they use Gast's laws to identify the fundamental objectives of the organization.

Before you conduct a value vote with your team, you will need to gather the following materials: a flip chart, a felt tip marker, and for each person on the team, five red stick-on dots, and three blue stick-on dots (You can buy these color stick-on dots at any office supply store). Once you have the materials, follow these steps:

1. Designate one member of the team as the facilitator (this is the role we assume when we work with client mission teams). The facilitator leads the group through the remaining steps.

2. Instruct the group to brainstorm for 15–30 minutes to develop an initial list of values. These can be either values that are currently part of the culture, or values that the team would like to see become part of the culture. When we did this exercise with the mission team for the School of Allied Health Professions, the team came up with this initial list of 40 values: *accessibility, accountability, appreciation for resources, citizenship, clear identity, cooperation, dedication, dignity, empowerment, encouragement, enjoyment, enthusiasm, equity, excellence in academics, financial fulfillment, flexibility, freedom, fulfillment of potential, globalistic, happiness, humor, innovation, integrity, integrity, love, loyalty, mentorship, personal growth, pride, quality product, respect for diversity, responsibility, reward, security, selfishness, sensitive, service, teamwork, unity, and urbanism.*

3. Write the list of values from step 2 on the flip chart, merging any duplicate values.

4. Give each team member five red dots and three blue dots.

5. *Red vote.* Invite each team member to walk up to the flip chart and to stick their red dots on the values that they feel are most important to the culture of the organization. You may stick one dot on five separate values, five dots on one value, or any combination in between. However, don't use your three blue dots yet.

6. Identify the 10–15 values that received the most votes during the red vote and cross out the rest. For the School of Allied Health Professions,

these 11 values survived the red vote with an arbitrary cutoff of at least 4 votes: *accountability, commitment, cooperation, dignity, enjoyment, excellence in academics, freedom, fulfillment of potential, innovation, integrity, and security.*

7. *Blue vote.* Repeat the vote, this time using the three blue dots on the values that survived the red vote.

8. Identify the 6–8 values that received the most votes in the blue vote and write these down on a clean flip chart sheet. For the School of Allied Health Professions, these values received the most blue votes, and became the list of shared values that helped guide the rest of the mission statement development: *enjoyment, excellence in academics, accountability, fulfillment of potential, cooperation, dignity, integrity, and innovation.*

After the value vote, lead the mission team in a discussion about the resulting list of values, and what the list reveals about the organization. Which values are a cherished part of the current culture? Which are not part of the culture but should be?

At the end of the session encourage the participants to write down the final list of values, and to keep these in mind as you use Gast's laws to develop the fundamental objectives for your organization.

We have found the value vote to be an excellent ice breaker. The technique can be used with almost any size group; we have used it with very small groups, and with groups as large as 267 participants (at a seminar in South Korea). In any case, the exercise usually takes only 30–40 minutes to finish. Appendix M contains some example values.

6.2   The group interview

Another technique that we use to help warm up the mission team is the *group interview*. This technique can extract a great deal of information from a group in a relatively short time. It helps identify concerns about mission statements in general, previous attempts to develop mission statements, and the upcoming effort to construct a new one. It can also help to build a sense of team and purpose among the members of the mission team.

The technical details of conducting a group interview are described in Appendix N. The basic idea is that the leader of the mission team poses a collection of questions, and then uses the group interview technique to get a summary of the team's answers to those questions. For example, here are some example questions that we pose when we conduct group interviews with mission teams:

1. Is it important for an organization to consider the mission statement during the planning process?

2. Is a mission statement important to this organization? Give one reason why or why not.

3. Will a good mission statement help improve the bottom line?

4. How long should it take for this organization to develop a strong sense of its mission.

5. What is the most serious obstacle the organization will face in trying to live the mission statement on a daily basis.

6. Is just having a mission statement enough to make it valuable?

7. Does the organization follow the ideals of the current mission statement?

8. Is it important to explain the organization's values in the mission statement?

9. What does it mean to manage a mission?

10. How should the organization change its behavior? Give one example.

Chapter 7

Use Gast's Laws to Identify Objectives

In the this step the mission team attempts to reach a consensus on the fundamental objectives that the organization should attempt to achieve in order to comply with Gast's laws.

There are two basic ways to organize this activity. The entire group can consider each law in turn, one after the other. Or the group can be divided into subgroups, the laws partitioned among these subgroups, and considered in parallel. There are advantages and disadvantages to each approach. Having the entire group consider each law has the advantage of a consistent treatment and understanding of all of the laws. The disadvantage is that it takes more time, which is a valuable resource in a busy organization. We've used both approaches successfully, so feel free to use the approach that makes the most sense for your situation.

The fundamental objectives that the mission team comes up with can be either new objectives or objectives that the organization already embraces. When we are working with a mission team on a particular law, we encourage the group to first produce a list of potential objectives, being careful to avoid any criticism or evaluation until everyone has made their suggestions. We typically write down all of the suggested objectives on tear sheets, and as the sheets fill up we attach them to the walls so that everyone can see them. Initially, the objectives don't have to be beautifully crafted sentences; sentence fragments or even individual words are OK at this stage. The important thing is to get as many suggestions as possible from the members of the group.

Once you have a complete list of suggested objectives, go over them one-by-one, discarding some, modifying others, and possibly adding new ones, until you arrive at the final list of objectives for that law. If you find yourselves deadlocked on some particular objective, discard it. Here are guidelines to help you develop the objectives for each law.

7.1   Objectives for Law 1

Law 1: A business must produce a want-satisfying commodity or service, and continually improve its ability to meet needs.

Law 1 consists of two parts. The first part addresses the need to clearly understand the core business of the organization, both now and in the future. The second part addresses the need for the organization to continually improve its ability to engage in its core business.

Without a doubt, Law 1 is the most important and difficult of the six laws to articulate clearly. You can expect the discussion for this law to take nearly as much time as the discussion for all of the other laws combined. Because of its importance, if you decide to break the mission team into separate parallel subgroups, then the head of the organization should be assigned to this subgroup.

Here are some basic questions to help you with the first part of Law 1:

1. What industry are we in?

2. What is our core business now?

3. What do we envision our core business being in the future?

4. Who are our customers?

5. Who are our competitors?

6. What geographic area do we serve?

7. How are we different from our competitors?

8. Where should we rank relative to our competitors?

Answering these questions will provide you with raw material that will help you describe precisely the core business of your organization.

For example, the School of Allied Health Professions came up with 10 major objectives for Law 1. Examples included producing competent allied health professionals, effectively representing and serving the departments in the school, facilitating distance learning, and fundraising. These were eventually summarized into the following general objectives: "The School of Allied Health Professionals serves as an international leader in the education of excellent, innovative, and responsible allied health professionals."

The VCU Department of Psychology came up with eight pages of material for Law 1, focusing on identifying their customers, the needs of those customers, and objectives that would satisfy those needs. These eight pages were eventually summarized in the following concise statement: "The Department of Psychology is a national leader promoting the understanding of behavior through the integration of scholarly inquiry, teaching, and service."

The basic lesson from these examples is that it is most effective to work from the specific towards the general. Start with a lot of detailed raw material, then condense and generalize into a small set of objectives that accurately represent the core business of your organization. Your objectives must be general enough so that they don't overwhelm with detail, but specific enough to accurately describe the business of your organization. Detailed objectives are better handled by conventional strategic planning processes rather than in mission statements.

Finding the proper balance between detail and generality can be difficult. Let's look at how the model mission statements in the appendices handle this tradeoff. The Anheuser-Busch Technology Acquisition Team aims "to provide key procurement services to Anheuser-Busch Companies, Inc. and its affiliates for all information technologies. These services include negotiation, risk management, vendor/product selection expertise, leadership in knowledge of industry trends, and other activities that promote the success of our customers." Notice how they identify the core business of the unit without limiting their options to find new markets.

British Airway's objective is to be the "undisputed leader in world travel." Notice that they don't say anything about airplanes. Rather, they view their core business as providing people with "world travel". While airplanes may be the best technology currently available for providing world travel, British Airways correctly views airplanes as a means to an end, rather than an end in themselves.

Ford Motor Company's statement of its core business is more precise, but still fairly general. "Ford Motor Company is a worldwide leader in automotive and automotive-related products and services as well as in newer industries such as aerospace, communications, and financial services."

Johnson & Johnson defines its core business as follows: "We believe our first responsibility is to the doctors, nurses and patients, to mothers and all others who use our products and services." Notice that Johnson & Johnson view their core business as meeting the needs of a certain group of customers, rather than producing specific products. While very general, this statement still manages to provide a clear notion of the purpose of the organization.

Ukrop's aims to be a "world-class provider of food and services." The view of providing services in addition to selling food is crucial, allowing for the possibility of expansion into new markets. In fact, Ukrop's has recently added banking and pharmacy services to its stores.

In almost every mission team that we work with, people suggest objectives that don't accurately reflect the core business of the organization. The group must be aware of this possibility and be willing to eliminate inappropriate objectives.

For example, we once had the opportunity to help the US Navy's Medical Service Corps develop a new mission statement. The Surgeon General of the Navy asked us to review a draft of the mission statement, and the following objective stood out like a sore thumb: "Our mission is to fight and win." It seemed to us as though the medical department shouldn't be doing any fighting, but rather supporting the fighting forces by providing the best possible medical care to them and their families. Our clients agreed, the mission was reworked, and the revised statement was adopted by Navy medical forces worldwide after being reviewed by over 900 people.

The second part of Law 1 focuses on the importance of continually improving the ability of the organization to engage in its core businesses. It is interesting that Prof. Gast was espousing the importance of continuous improvement at the same time that W. Edwards Deming was advocating a similar approach in Japan in the 1950's. Mr. Deming's ideas were not accepted in this country until the early 1980's, but since then they have had a tremendous impact on American industry and its subsequent success.

Unfortunately, mission statements usually skip this important part of Law 1. However, it is extremely rare to find a successful company that doesn't continually improve its ability to meet customer needs. Thus we rarely have a problem getting our clients to agree on the need for continual improvement, and including a statement to that effect in their mission statement.

For example, the Anheuser-Busch Technology Acquisition Team has a "fundamental commitment to continuous improvement of our services, targeted to ultimately achieve customer delight." British Airways is mum on the need for continuous improvement. Ford Motor, on the other hand, is quite clear: "Our mission is to improve continuously our products and services to meet our customer's needs." Also, "continuous improvement is essential to our success. We must strive for excellence in everything we do." Johnson & Johnson elegantly addresses the need for continuous improvement: "We must experiment with new ideas. Research must be carried on, innovative programs developed and mistakes paid for. New equipment must be purchased, new facilities provided and new products launched." Ukrop's recognizes the importance of "minimizing waste and vigorously pursuing continuous improvement". The School of Allied Health Professions "nurtures continuous growth in their knowledge base and productivity". Similarly for the VCU Department of Psychology: "We achieve excellence by continuously measuring our performance and productivity as scholars, teachers, contributors to society, and as a Department in order to effectively meet the changing needs of our consumers, whether they be students, staff, faculty, the Commonwealth of Virginia, or society." This, by the way, is an unusual and powerful commitment by an academic mission statement to improve productivity.

In sum, Law 1 is the most difficult of the six laws for a mission team to articulate clearly and to reach a consensus on. And yet it is extremely important because it involves understanding the core business of the organization.

Peter Drucker claims that most business people do not know what business they are in. We have found that most managers feel that they understand the purpose of their business. However, when asked to actually write it down, they often struggle, because articulating the purpose of a business involves a more in-depth generic inspection of what the organization does.

For example, in the mid 1990's European airline executives were asking the following question, "Is our business flying airplanes or arranging transportation?" Airlines already outsource food service, and lease of airplanes. Will they someday outsource pilots, baggage handling, cargo and flight attendants? Bertrand d'Yvoire, president of Consultair in Paris, contends that "an airline's real business is managing reservation and traffic systems." The key to the thinking involved here is to go beneath the surface of the organization's apparent business, and to look at fundamentals.

As another example, when we examine the generally excellent mission statements of the Baldrige Award winners, we find that we can easily understand the overall purpose of the organizations, but cannot usually identify the particular products that the organizations produce. For instance, consider the Solectron mission statement: "With integrity and ethical business practices, provide worldwide responsiveness to our customers with the highest quality, lowest total cost, customized integrated manufacturing services through long term partnerships."

Gast defined the requirement to improve our ability to meet needs in 1952. Is this still required? Have times changed so much that these societal requirements no longer apply? We believe that knowing what our business is, to continually improve, to be kind to the environment and have respect for people, and other laws defined by Gast, are as essential today as ever. Global competition, millisecond communication, advanced technology and productive capacity don't change these societal requirements. And in fact, they are more important today than ever. We have the capacity to do more positive things than we have ever had. We also have the capacity to injure more people, more quickly, to do more damage to the local and global economy, the environment and society than ever.

Interestingly, many people make the mistake of using the mission statement to describe the core business of the organization, and nothing more. However, organizations have other responsibilities besides conducting their core business, and a good mission statement will address these as well. The next sections describe some of these responsibilities and how they can be incorporated in a mission statement.

7.2   Objectives for Law 2

> *Law 2: A business must increase the wealth or quality of life of society through the economic use of labor and capital.*

This law, like the previous one, consists of two parts. The first part addresses the obligation of a business to contribute to society in general, and to the communities where it does business in particular. By requiring that the organization make economic use of labor and capital as it increases the wealth of society, the second part of Law 2 tells us that employees — both workers and managers — have an obligation to ensure that the organization produces high quality goods or services cost-effectively.

Here are some questions to help you identify objectives for the first part of Law 2:

1. How does our organization help or hurt the community?

2. Should we be doing more to help?

3. Should we be doing less to hurt?

Almost every organization has some positive impact on their communities and their societies. Some organizations may have negative effects such as pollution, bribery, or political corruption. A thoughtful and honest assessment of the positive and negative impacts of your organization is a fascinating and important exercise.

The notion of a business making a contribution to its community and its society resonates strongly with the mission teams we have worked with in the past. As one participant told us, "If my company helps the community, then by my participation in the work of the organization, I too am helping the community. I am proud of this contribution."

If an organization does not take a clear proactive stance, it probably will not do much, if anything, that it isn't required to by law and regulation. The mission statement is where an organization can decide to be proactive and to make a positive difference to society and the community. In particular, the issue of the environment is becoming increasingly important in modern mission statements.

Recognition of the obligation to society and community appears in all of our model mission statements.

According to the Anheuser-Busch Technology Acquisition Team: "Our contribution to the quality of life is to promote the organization's responsibilities for our impact on the environment and society." British Airways wants to be a "global and caring good neighbor." Ford Motor recognizes that "the conduct of our company worldwide must be pursued in a manner that is socially responsible and commands respect for its integrity and for its positive contributions to society."

Johnson & Johnson devotes a major part of its mission statement to societal responsibilities: "We are responsible to the communities in which we live and work and to the world community as well. We must be good citizens - support good works and charities and bear our fair share of taxes. We must encourage civic improvements and better health and education. We must maintain in good order the property we are privileged to use, protecting the environment and natural resources." This is incredibly enlightened, especially given that most of it was written over 50 years ago.

Ukrop's notes that "the mission of Ukrop's is to serve our customers and community", and also recognizes the need for "improving the lives of our families and well-being of our community." The VCU Department of Psychology aims to "lead the way in improving the quality of life in society through the development of knowledge and technology, finding ways of addressing human problems, and educating people to be responsible citizens and effective leaders." The School of Allied Health Professions recognizes that "the School, responsive to the needs of society, promotes excellence in health care service."

The second part of Law 2 addresses the responsibility of employees to be as productive as possible, producing high quality products cost-effectively. Gast was addressing what we usually refer to today as quality control or quality management. A commitment to quality and productivity improvement should appear in every mission statement.

The issue of productivity and quality improvement is already important to most industrial businesses, and it should be a high priority for all organizations, including churches, schools, government and non-profit organizations. Gast's intent with the second part of Law 2 is to recognize the responsibilities of both managers and workers to improve productivity. Managers must provide an environment that promotes productivity and workers must work hard and smart within that environment.

Most of our model mission statements do a good job of recognizing the importance of quality and productivity.

The Anheuser-Busch Technology Acquisition Team vows that "our commitment in providing our services is to be *the best* — efficient, effective, and constantly improving our ability to meet or exceed our customers' expectations." They also recognize the importance of "providing our customers with the highest ideals of timeliness, accuracy, consistency, and completeness in our work." British Airways aims for "superior value in world travel."

Ford Motor refers to quality and productivity again and again in their mission statement, promising "to improve continually our products and services to meet our customers' needs, allowing us to prosper as a business and to provide a reasonable return for our stockholders, the owners of our business." Ford also believes that "Quality comes first — To achieve customer satisfaction, the quality of our products and services must be our number one priority." In the Ford view, profits are tied directly to quality: "Profits are the ultimate measure of how efficiently we provide customers with the best products for their needs. Profits are required to survive and grow." And we also see a strong commitment to the customer: "Customers are the focus of everything we do — Our work must be done with our customers in mind, providing better products and services than our competition."

Johnson & Johnson states that "in meeting their needs everything we do must be of high quality. We must constantly strive to reduce our costs in order to maintain reasonable prices. Customers' orders must be serviced promptly and accurately." Ukrop's promises to "provide the greatest value possible by offering a wide variety and excellent service, while fulfilling our customers' desire for high quality, uncompromising freshness, and low prices." Ukrop's also values "minimizing waste and vigorously pursuing productivity improvements." The School of Allied Health Professions "nurtures continuous growth in their knowledge base and productivity." The VCU Department of Psychology maintains that "in all our endeavors, we strive to use resources cost-effectively."

To summarize, Law 2 describes the obligations of a business to its community and society in general, and the obligations of its employees to produce quality goods or services cost-effectively. Law 2 is interesting because it recognizes that the obligation to be productive is a two-way street. The organization must provide appropriate management, systems, and resources. Employees must work hard to make the best use of the resources they are given.

7.3 Objectives for Law 3

Law 3: A business must provide opportunities for the productive employment of people.

Law 3 is the most controversial of Gast's laws, and yet it is probably the most important because it defines the basic relationship between an organization and its employees. Law 3 says that a business is not required to hire people it doesn't need, but if and when it does hire them, it assumes an obligation to work as hard as possible to keep them productively employed.

In an organization that really practices Law 3, employees are respected and valued by the organization. They are not disposable parts that can be flushed whenever it is expedient. So while on the surface, Law 3 is about providing productive employment for people, at its core it is about creating a work environment where people trust and respect each other. For this reason, when we work with mission groups on Law 3, we focus on these values of trust and respect for people.

Valuing people is a relatively new principle in management, and Gast was way ahead of his time in this respect. Unfortunately, there are still many organizations that do not practice the values of trust and respect embodied in Law 3. Scott Adams's Dilbert cartoon strip derives its humor and its legions of fans from companies who don't follow Law 3.

The basic claim of Law 3 is that companies that care for their employees will do better in the long term than those that do not. We can't prove this assertion, but we can offer some anecdotal evidence from our own observations and experience.

When Prof. Steven Robbins was appointed as chair of the VCU Department of Psychology, the department was in difficult straits, with a long history of unhappy faculty. As one of his first tasks, Prof. Robbins used our method to implement a new departmental mission based on respect, trust, and fairness.

He reorganized the work load of the faculty so that responsibilities were evenly divided. He gave credit to faculty who were making a significant contribution to the department, and counseled those who were not. The faculty adopted a system of annual reviews that was comprehensive and fair, and included professional improvement plans and goals. In spite of the fact that these changes caused some unhappiness and even defections, his rating by the faculty went up each year. We believe that this happened because he cared for the people in his department, he established a reasonable level of expected discipline, and created an environment that treated people fairly.

As another example, a small section in a large financial organization had a long history of unhappy workers whose work was error-prone, and whose productivity was the lowest of any comparable section in the organization.

One of the corporate vice presidents, Dave Thomas, was put in charge of the section and told to clean out the entire work group, and to rehire and train new people. Instead, he first looked at the people and their problems. He could see they suffered from lack of direction and goals. So Mr. Thomas used our method to develop a new mission for the section that spoke of mutual respect and he helped the existing employees develop a simple work improvement effort. The end result was that within six months the section behaved quite differently. The desks throughout the office had been rearranged to improve communication and the flow of work. The employees felt good about themselves and each other. Communications improved. New simplified systems were developed. Productivity went up dramatically, and the section eventually became the most productive in the company.

Another example in a different industry involved a small 5-person section of a large company. Again, it was taken over by a new leader who found the morale and productivity of the people in poor shape. Using our method, the new section leader worked with the employees to develop a new mission statement, and he began using the mission statement in his decision making. The statement emphasized how important the people in the department were, and how innovation was an expected behavior. The end result was that both morale and productivity improved throughout the section. Service to the internal customers this section served was improved and recognized. In three years, the section grew from 5 people to 25 people, in recognition of its increased value to the company.

It is not easy to create an environment based on trust and respect, even with the best of intentions. In the mid 1980s, Dick O'Hallaron was a regional vice president for a large health care organization. In addition to his own unit, he was responsible for three other operations with about 3,000 employees. One of these units underwent a solicitation by union organizers. When Dick chartered an outside firm to conduct an employee survey to learn how management was perceived by the employees, the results showed a number of problems. In particular, it appeared to the employees that management did not care about them. This was not true, but the perception was there nonetheless. The CEO took some immediate steps to correct this perception and in the end the union was not voted in by the employees.

After this incident Dick began to wonder about the way that the 1,200 employees in his own unit felt about management. He had always tried to create an environment based on trust and respect for people and was confident that there wasn't a similar problem in his own unit. But just to be sure, he asked the same outfit to do a similar survey of his own organization. To his dismay, the results of the survey were almost identical to the unit that had the union problems. He took corrective action and eventually fixed the problem, but it is interesting to realize that good intentions are not always enough.

The objectives for Law 3 do not need to be detailed. But they must convey a strong sense of interest and respect for the people in the organization.

For example, the Anheuser-Busch Technology Acquisition Team stresses "the fundamental respect and dignity for each individual with whom we have contact in the pursuit of our vision." British Airways recognizes the need for its people to be "safe and secure", to be a "caring good neighbor", and to have " inspired teams of people building and benefiting from the company's success, sharing a cause, feeling good about working together and delighting the customer." Ford Motor emphasizes the importance of people with this statement: "Our people are the source of our strength. They provide our corporate intelligence and determine our reputation and vitality." Johnson & Johnson states that "we are responsible to our employees, the men and women who work with us throughout the world. Everyone must be considered as an individual. We must respect their dignity and recognize their merit. They must have a sense of security in their jobs." Ukrop's recognizes the importance of "treating our customers, associates, and suppliers as we personally would like to be treated." The VCU Dept. of Psychology emphasizes the importance of mutual respect: "We value and refuse to devalue other people, including our staff, faculty, students, members of our University community, and all other constituents." The School of Allied Health Professions promises to "respect the value and uniqueness of each individual."

Unfortunately, mission statements often fail to address Law 3. In 1996 and 1997, we did a survey of the mission statements from academic marketing departments. Of the 90 departments contacted, 40 furnished their mission statements. Most of these statements focused on faculty, but few mentioned anything about the other employees in the department. As another example, the mission statement for Virginia Commonwealth University speaks of students and faculty, but is silent on the issue of non-faculty employees.

The ideas in Law 3 of trust and respect for people also apply to the suppliers, vendors, and contractors that do business with the organization.

While they are often ignored in mission statements, we find that the really good organizations remember these people as well.

For example, the Anheuser-Busch Technology Acquisition Team promises "to do our best to respect our vendors and their investments of time and resources. We will treat them fairly and honestly in striving to award our business based on excellent service, superior quality, and competitive price. We intend to build long-term relationships with the best suppliers in the industry." Johnson & Johnson believes that "our suppliers and distributors must have an opportunity to make a fair profit." Ford Motor recognizes that "Dealers and suppliers are our partners. The company must maintain mutually beneficial relationships with dealers, suppliers, and our other business associates." Ukrop's states that "The mission of Ukrop's is to serve our customers and community efficiently and effectively while treating our customers, associates, and suppliers as we personally like to be treated."

In sum, Law 3 is crucial (and controversial) because it describes a fundamental relationship between an organization and its employees, contractors, and suppliers that is based on trust and respect. Every mission statement should speak directly to these key values of trust and respect.

7.4 Objectives for Law 4

Law 4: A business must provide opportunities for the satisfaction of normal occupational desires.

Law 4 embodies the same themes of trust and respect that we found in Law 3. The basic premise of Law 4 is that people take their job seriously and want to do it well. Law 4 reminds us of an organization's responsibility to help employees learn, grow, and excel in their jobs; to be the best employees that they can be.

The idea behind Law 4 is to recognize the obligation of the organization to create a *great quality of work life* for the employees. In an organization with a great quality of work life, people enjoy coming to work and participating in the activities and goals of the organization. Such a place will have its own built-in quality improvement program, carried on by employees who want to see the organization improve and succeed.

Unlike the first three laws we have studied, Law 4 tends to be easy for most mission teams to understand and articulate, mainly because it is concrete and relates directly to every employee's experience. The basic questions to ask during this session are:

1. What are we doing to help employees learn and grow in their jobs?

2. What aren't we doing that we should be doing?

When answering these questions, mission teams typically discuss issues such as career development, training, challenging work, comfort, working environment, communications, empowerment, recognition, safety, and training. When we work with our clients on this law, we find that about half of the objectives suggested by the mission team pertain to the good things that the organization is already doing, and the other half to the things that the group wishes the organization would do, but doesn't.

We have never seen a mission team get stuck for material for this law. However, it is important not to turn things into a gripe session. If the organization is lacking in certain areas, identify and agree on objectives that address these failings in a general sense, and then move on.

The Anheuser-Busch Technology Acquisition Team notes the importance of "recognizing the contributions of our team members and providing them with opportunities for satisfying and financially rewarding work with continuous opportunities for personal development and advancement." British Airways wants "inspired teams of people building and benefiting from the company's success, sharing a cause, feeling good about working together and delighting the customer." Notice how this statement covers both Laws 3 and 4.

At Ford Motor there is a belief that "involvement and teamwork are our core human values. Employee involvement is our way of life. We are a team. We must treat each other with trust and respect." Johnson & Johnson is adamant in their desire to provide a good environment for their employees: "Everyone must be considered as an individual. We must respect their dignity and recognize their merit. They must have a sense of security in their jobs. Employees must fee free to make suggestions and complaints. There must be equal opportunity for employment, development and advancement of those qualified. We must provide competent management, and their actions must be just and ethical." Ukrop's aims for the following for its employees (associates): "For our associates, we will promote a pleasant and challenging work environment where work can be an enjoyable experience.

We will give our associates an opportunity to grow and advance according to their proven abilities and demonstrated desire to improve themselves professionally."

The School of Allied Health Professions devotes a large part of their mission statement to Law 4:

- Cooperation — We collaborate through the practice of open communication, trust, and respect.

- Enjoyment — We value internal well-being, creative enrichment, and a spirit of joyfulness.

- Excellence — We practice and promote the highest standard of quality performance and care of the individual.

- Fulfillment of potential — We facilitate continual professional development and personal growth.

- Innovation — We encourage and support creativity.

The VCU Dept. of Psychology states that "Our work is created with excellence, conceived in wisdom, and aimed at improving the quality of life. Our productivity is maintained in an environment of fairness, mutual respect, and enjoyment."

In sum, the idea behind Law 4 is to recognize the need to create a great environment for people to work, to help them develop professionally, and to be the best employees that they can be.

7.5   Objectives for Law 5

Law 5: A business must provide just wages for labor.

This is a relatively easy law to understand and articulate; we all know that we should be paid more! However, we have a few suggestions that might be helpful.

Compensation is a sensitive issue, but it must be mentioned in the mission statement nonetheless. Employees need to know that the organization is committed to paying them just wages. We have seen a number of mission statements that did not address the issue of just compensation because management felt this was their right alone, and they did not want employees or anyone else interfering.

A common question is what to do when the mission team represents an organization such as a business department/section or government agency that doesn't control the wage and salary structure. In these cases, we recommend still addressing Law 5 in the mission statement, if only to say that the department or section will advocate for fair compensation for its employees.

Providing fair compensation to all people that an organization deals with, including employees, vendors, and subcontractors, is completely consistent with the notion of respect for people embodied in Laws 3 and 4. Thus we find commitments to providing just compensation to vendors, suppliers, and contractors becoming more commonplace in mission statements. For example:

The Anheuser-Busch Technology Acquisition Team promises that "we will do our best to respect our vendors and their investments of time and resources. We will treat them fairly and honestly in striving to award our business based on excellent service, superior quality and competitive price." They also acknowledge the importance of "recognizing the contributions of our team members and providing them with opportunities for satisfying and financially rewarding work." British Airways wants its employees "benefiting from the company's success." Ford Motor is silent on the issue of compensation. Johnson & Johnson states that "compensation must be fair and adequate." Ukrop's "will fairly compensate our associates for their performance and they will share in the success of the company through profit-sharing bonuses. To our suppliers, we will do our best to provide a fair return on their investments of time and resources." The VCU Dept. of Psychology is quite up front: "We advocate fair compensation, and seek creative means of developing and managing compensation for our people and Department." The School of Allied Health Professions claims that "the School fosters fair and equitable work responsibilities and compensation."

In sum, compensation is a tricky subject and not easy to agree on. However, Law 5 tells us that an organization should recognize the importance of fair compensation and always strive towards that goal.

7.6   Objectives for Law 6

Law 6: A business must provide a just return on capital.

Law 6 is straightforward with respect to for-profit businesses: the organization should return a reasonable return on the investments of its owners. But what does it mean for organizations like schools, non-profit businesses, churches, and government agencies?

In fact, Law 6 applies to these organizations as well. They merely have different notions of return on capital. The idea of Law 6 is that an organization must make good use of the money that funds the organization, whether this money is in the form of stockholder investments, private investments, tuition, or taxes.

For example, a school is obligated by Law 6 to provide a good education to students in return for the tuition and taxes that they and their parents pay to fund the school. Government agencies must also work hard to provide cost-effective service to the taxpayers who provide their operating budgets. Corporate research labs must help provide new product ideas to the business units that fund them. Similarly, departments or sections that receive budgets from a larger organization have an obligation to use their budgets wisely.

It is surprising how many organizations omit this important law from their mission statements. However, here is how our model mission statements addressed Law 6.

The Anheuser-Busch Technology Acquisition Team vows to "insure a superior return on the investment of our company has made in our team, by striving to add value, eliminate waste and achieve the lowest total system cost for our customers." British Airways simply wants to "enjoy strong profitability." Johnson & Johnson is brief and explicit: "When we operate according to these principles, the stockholders should realize a fair return."

Ukrop's Super Markets acknowledges the importance of "long term profitability and growth — a measure of success which associates share through bonuses and new opportunities" and also hopes to "achieve profitable growth and long-term financial success." Ford Motor aims to "prosper as a business and to provide a reasonable return for our stockholders, the owners of our business." Ford also recognizes the importance of profits as "the ultimate measure of how efficiently we provide customers with the best products for their needs. Profits are required to survive and grow."

The VCU Dept. of Psychology promises that "in all our endeavors, we strive to use resources cost-effectively so that we can best achieve this mission and the missions of the College of Humanities and Sciences and of Virginia Commonwealth University." The School of Allied Health Professions "recognizes the importance of being accountable to the students and their families, the Commonwealth, faculty, staff, alumni, and other benefactors by using resources effectively."

Many Catholic hospitals address Law 6 using statements focusing on stewardship responsibilities.

In sum, Law 6 applies to any organization, even churches, schools, and non-profit institutions such as hospitals and charities. Every organization requires capital in order to survive, and every investor deserves a reasonable return. Of course, different kinds of organizations will have different notions of return on capital and what comprises a just return.

Chapter 8

Construct the Mission Statement

To this point you have considered each of Gast's laws, and for each law have identified a set of fundamental objectives for your organization. In this third step, the mission team hands over this set of fundamental objectives to the *mission writers* — a subgroup of the original mission team chaired by the head of the organization — who then use these objectives as the raw material from which they craft the mission statement.

This step is somewhat of an art, and depends a great deal on the taste and writing ability of the mission writers. However, there are some identifiable styles, and we'll use examples of existing mission statements to describe these different approaches.

If developed properly, the list of objectives handed over to the mission writers will address each of Gast's laws. For example, the mission team for the VCU Department of Psychology handed over the following raw material to their mission writers:

1. Promote understanding of behavior [Law 1].

2. Promote an environment conducive to learning [Law 1].

3. Promote our traditional commitment to applied societally relevant psychology [Law 1].

4. Measure effectiveness of curriculum goals against goals of students, undergraduate, post-graduate students, and use the information to improve the curriculum and process [Law 1].

5. Take effective measures to enhance classroom experiences for faculty and students [Law 1].

6. Improve the quality of life in society through the development of knowledge, technology, finding effective ways of addressing human problems, providing educated citizens and ethical leaders and citizens [Law 2].

7. Carry out annual evaluations of faculty and staff, focused in part on productivity in various areas [Law 2].

8. Enhance mechanisms for the recognition of people's work [Law 3].

9. Provide equitable and fair access to professional growth and advancement [Law 4].

10. Advocate for fair compensation and be creative in developing and managing a fair wage and salary effort [Law 5].

11. Improve the quality of life after graduation [Law 6].

The job of the mission writers is to compose this list of objectives into a mission statement. This process is a matter of taste and style. There are no hard and fast rules, but existing mission statements do tend to follow a few general approaches.

8.1   Styles of mission statements

One approach is to write the mission statement as a sequence of complete sentences, where each sentence describes one or more of the objectives supplied by the mission team. Of course a great deal of wordsmithing of the original objectives is likely, but the basic idea is to simply compose these reworded objectives in some order. Johnson & Johnson use this approach very effectively in their elegant mission statement (see Appendix G). The Johnson & Johnson statement is interesting because it simply lists the various responsibilities of the organization to its employees, suppliers, investors, and community.

Other organizations partition their objectives into separate sections with headings such as *Vision*, *Mission*, *Goals*, *Values*, and *Guiding Principles*.

How the objectives are partitioned into sections and how these sections are entitled is entirely at the discretion of the mission writers. We don't know of any precise definitions for the different sections, and it's probably not worth the effort to try to define them. In general, though, sections with titles like *Mission*, *Vision*, and *Goals* tend to include objectives related to the organization's core business, productivity, and financial performance (Laws 1 and 6). We refer to these as *business objectives*.

On the other hand, sections with titles like *Values* and *Guiding Principles* tend to relate to objectives that describe how the organization intends to behave as it engages in its core business (Laws 2, 3, 4, and 5). We refer to these as *behavioral objectives*.

The British Airways mission statement is an example of a mission statement that partitions its objectives into separate sections. The business objectives are listed in the *Mission* and *Goals* sections. The behavioral objectives are listed in the *Values* section. Addendum O has a list of values, or behavioral objectives with descriptions of the expected behavior.

Another common approach is to first list *all* of the objectives in one section, followed by a second section that emphasizes the values or beliefs that are implied by the behavioral objectives listed in the first section. For example, the *Vision* section of the VCU Department of Psychology's mission statement is quite clear about the Department's commitment to helping students learn and to helping employees grow professionally and to be paid fairly. These objectives imply that the people in the department share values such as productivity, excellence, mutual respect, and fairness. These shared values are repeated and highlighted in a separate *Values* section.

Again, the decision to use separate sections is a matter of taste. In practice, most modern mission statements do use separate sections to highlight the organization's values, for several reasons. First, a new or revised mission statement is often used as a management tool to help change some aspect of an organization's culture (more on this in the next chapter). Since the culture is summarized by the organization's behavioral objectives, mission writers will often highlight and emphasize new values proposed by the mission team. Second, the mission statement is also used as a sales tool to help attract new employees, contractors, vendors, and customers. Mission writers will often highlight shared values that they think will be attractive to these groups.

In our experience, when the objectives for Laws 2–5 are done correctly, they always reflect the shared values of respect for people, mutual trust, and the importance of quality. We believe strongly that if you do choose to highlight your organization's values, the list should include these three crucial values.

8.2   All mission statements are not alike!

Another important issue is to ensure that the final mission statement reflects the special nature of the organization. We don't want a mission statement to be boilerplate that could be applied anywhere.

For example, we once worked on the mission statement for a Catholic welfare agency. When the local bishop reviewed the final document, his reaction was, "This doesn't look like a church sponsored agency. This could be a welfare agency sponsored by any group. What you have done is secularize the statement. There is no mention of the healing ministry of Jesus. There is no mention of the focus of our faith or the important and necessary spiritual dimensions of this organization."

He was right of course. Churches and church groups need mission statements, and their statements should conform to Gast's laws like those of any other organization. But in describing the objectives, we need to keep in mind the unique nature of the organization and make sure that the objectives are not too generic.

Andrew Campbell, Director of the Ashridge Strategic Management Centre in London, England, and one of the most prolific writers on the subject of organizational mission, emphasizes the importance of a mission statement being unique to the organization.

Writes Dr. Campbell, "One of the difficulties of mission statements is making them idiosyncratic. One professor used to ask his manager students to give him a copy of their company's mission before class. He then read out the first one, omitting the company's name and asked who's it was. He claimed that at least half of those who had handed in statements raised their hands."

Dr. Campbell is absolutely right about the need to make mission statements unique. Gast's laws do not imply that you simply write a standard mission statement, like a model legal document, and fill in the blanks that are left for your company's name and business focus. Your mission statement must speak to the unique nature of your organization.

8.3 The review process

In our experience, successful efforts to write mission statements include an extensive review process. The review process is an iterative one that goes through several review/modify cycles, with reviews from the mission team itself, upper management, and the rest of the organization.

A typical cycle would be to request comments from the rest of the mission team, make necessary changes, request comments on the modified version, make more changes, and so on, until the mission group reaches a consensus on the document. This draft is then distributed to an appropriate cross-section of the organization for review and comments. Finally, the final draft of the mission statement should be approved by the appropriate higher authority. For example, if the mission statement is for an entire company, then it should be approved by the board of directors. If the statement is for a section, then it should be approved by the section head's boss.

The VCU Dept. of Psychology sent a draft of their mission statement to every faculty member and employee in the Department for review. Similarly, by the time the mission statement for the School of Allied Health Professions was adopted, over 80 people had been involved as either members of the mission team, mission writers, or reviewers. Finally, the U.S. Navy Medical Service Corps sent a draft of their mission statement to over 900 members of the corps worldwide for review before the final version was published.

The important idea in the review process is to expose the mission statement to as many people as possible, and to get as many people as possible to buy in to the proposed statement before it is officially adopted. Achieving this kind of acceptance is crucial because it allows the mission statement to become a useful tool that plays an active role in the day-to-day operation of the organization. If people in the organization don't know about the mission statement or don't accept it, then of course it will have little value. But if you have followed our suggestions and based the mission statement on Gast's laws, then we can almost guarantee that the mission statement will be accepted by the people in your organization, and that it will be effective.

How real managers in real companies use their mission statements on a day-to-day basis is the topic of step 4, which is described in the next chapter.

8.4   Frequently asked questions

Here are some questions that people frequently ask when they are constructing a mission statement. We have already addressed them in previous sections, but the questions come up so often that we think it is helpful to explicitly list them:

Q1: *If we base our mission statement on Gast's laws, won't it look the same as every other mission statement based on Gast's laws?*

A1: No! Consider the following analogy. If you were to X-ray 100 people their skeletal formation would look quite similar. You'd see bones of hands, legs, body and skull. Similarly, if you were to X-ray (analyze) 100 good mission statements you would find that in general they have very similar objectives (i.e., Gast's laws).

Now put some flesh on the skeleton bones and the differences quickly become apparent. Men look much different than women. Some people have blue eyes, others brown. Some have blond hair, others black or brown hair. Some have light skin, others various shades of darker skin. Then add a mind, personality and behavior to the skeleton and differences become even more apparent.

A mission statement is similar. Although most good statements have a similar skeleton, each can and should be described in a way that puts a special emphasis on what the organization does and how it intends to behave. It must have some meat on the bones to give it a distinctive personality.

To illustrate this point with a real (and great) mission statement, consider the Johnson & Johnson Credo, which is clearly unique, and yet neatly addresses each of Gast's laws (and nothing more!). Every sentence in this statement can be associated with one of Gast's laws:

Law 1 is addressed by the following sentences (note that they are taken out of order from the Johnson & Johnson Credo):

We believe our first responsibility is to the doctor, nurses and patients,
to mothers and all others who use our products and services.
. . .
Customers' orders must be serviced promptly and accurately.
. . .
We must experiment with new ideas.
Research must be carried on, innovative programs developed
and mistakes paid for.
New equipment must be purchased, new facilities provided
and new products launched.

Law 2 is addressed by the following parts:

In meeting their needs everything we do must be of high quality.
. . .
We must constantly strive to reduce our costs
in order to maintain reasonable prices.
. . .
We must provide competent management,
and their actions must be just and ethical. We are responsible to the
communities in which we live and work
and to the world community as well.
We must be good citizens - support good works and charities
and bear our fair share of taxes.
We must encourage civic improvements and better health and education.
We must maintain in good order
the property we are privileged to use,
protecting the environment and natural resources.

Law 3 is addressed by the following:

Our suppliers and distributors must have an opportunity
to make a fair profit. We are responsible to our employees,
the men and women who work with us throughout the world.
Everyone must be considered as an individual.
We must respect their dignity and recognize their merit.

Law 4 is covered by the following statements:

They must have a sense of security in their jobs.

. . .

and working conditions clean, orderly and safe.
We must be mindful of ways to help our employees fulfill
their family responsibilities.
Employees must feel free to make suggestions and complaints.
There must be equal opportunity for employment, development
and advancement for those qualified.

Law 5 is addressed by the following:

Compensation must be fair and adequate,

And Law 6 is addressed by the following:

Our final responsibility is to our stockholders.
Business must make a sound profit.

. . .

Reserves must be created to provide for adverse times.
When we operate according to these principles,
the stockholders should realize a fair return.

With its narrative prose style, the Johnson & Johnson statement mission is quite different from any other mission statement we have seen. Yet it contains all the generic features of Gast's laws (although of course Gast's laws hadn't yet been invented when the Johnson & Johnson mission statement was coined). See Section 8.2 for a discussion on making your mission statement unique.

Q2: *We see mission statements with different parts labeled "Mission", "Vision", "Values", "Quality goals", and so on. Which of these parts is the mission?*

A2: They all are! See Section 8.1 for a discussion of the different parts of a mission statement.

Q3: *People tell me that mission statements must be short enough to be memorized. Is this true?*

A3: Not necessarily. It must be long enough to describe how the organization intends to comply with Gast's laws, no more and no less. For example,

Ukrop's mission has 216 words, Johnson & Johnson has 308 words, British Airways has 129 words, and Ford Motor Company has 358 words. These excellent mission statement are probably too long for most of us to memorize, but many of Ukrop's employees do indeed memorize their mission statement. However, the main goal should always be to develop a mission statement that is an effective management tool.

Q4: *We know what our mission is. Why do we need to write it down?*

A4: Because you can't be sure that the people in the organization really understand the mission until you write it down. Often, ideas that seem clear in our heads are exposed as being murky, incomplete, or contradictory when we try to put them to paper.

Chapter 9

Use the Mission Statement

To this point, you have worked hard to create a good mission statement based on Gast's laws. But there are many good mission statements that hang forgotten on the wall and play no role in the daily life of the organization. So how do you turn your *good* mission statement into an *effective* one that is used regularly and strategically?

This chapter contains examples of organizations whose mission statements play a powerful role in the daily life of the organization. It is our hope that these examples from real organizations will give you some ideas for making your mission statement an effective tool. We think that real examples will be much more helpful to you than any theories we might have on how to make effective use of your mission statement.

Some of the stories are based on our own business. Others come from managers from a variety of successful organizations. The organizations include a small section in a giant multinational, a mid-sized regional firm, some university departments, and a health care system. Here are their stories.

9.1   Anheuser-Busch Technology Acquisition Team

The Anheuser-Busch Technology Acquisition Team is a group of about 25 people who negotiate contracts for computer and communication equipment and who hire contract programmers for Anheuser-Busch, the world's leading beer manufacturer. Gary Foster, the team manager, led the development of the mission statement, using Gast's laws, in 1994. According to Mr.

Foster, the mission statement has played an active role in that growth, and it continues to play an important role in the daily business of the group.

Mr. Foster and his group use the mission statement to drive their strategic planning process. In particular, they use the mission statement to identify a set of long-term goals that they call "mission targets". These mission targets are long term goals that are implied by the objectives contained in their mission statement. Each year, they try to figure out how to get closer to these mission targets, and make plans, broken down in quarterly phases, including time tables, measurable activities, and specific responsibilities.

The team also uses the mission statement to help with daily and strategic problem solving. When they are assigned a new function as part of a reorganization, they look at the new function and determine if it fits into the core business defined in their mission statement: the purchasing of all information technologies for Anheuser-Busch. If it doesn't fit, then they attempt to have the work transferred out of their section.

For example, in one case the team inherited a security function for promoting mainframe programs to production status from test status. This function took the majority of one person's time, but was inconsistent with the team's mission. There were two alternatives: (1) transfer the person out of the group, or (2) automate the function so the person could work on more appropriate tasks. The group chose the latter option, automated the task, and put the person to work on other tasks that were more consistent with the team's mission.

As another example, during one consolidation phase the group was given the job of hiring consultants for the information service area. There was a question initially about whether this new role was consistent with the mission of the group. However, a reflection on the mission statement revealed a good fit, and they were able to integrate the new role smoothly into their operation.

On the other hand, they also use their mission statement to identify functions being performed elsewhere that should be handled by their group. For example, at one point, the outsourcing of some computer programming work to an offshore firm was being handled by another group within the company. However, since it fit so well into their core business, they were able to campaign successfully to incorporate the outsourcing function into their group.

Mr. Foster also uses the mission statement in developing relations with vendors, suppliers, internal customers, and employees. He includes a copy of the mission statement in the service agreements for internal customers, as well as in the purchasing guide for vendors. He displays mission statements in his office, in the group's conference room, on the story board outside the office, and on the group's Web page. He gives a copy to each employee, reviews it with each employee candidate, and uses it to counsel employees. Finally, he uses the mission statement to encourage his employees to make suggestions and to disagree with him when they think it is important.

9.2 Ukrop's Super Markets

Ukrop's is a world class grocery chain in the Richmond, VA area. The company is written about regularly in business journals, and executives from throughout Europe, Great Britain, South America and the Far East visit Ukrop's stores on a regular basis to learn about their operation.

According to Jim Ukrop, President, their mission statement was developed in 1988 as part of the 50th anniversary celebration of the company's founding. It has been an integral part of their day-to-day operation ever since, with only minor changes. Their mission statement is an important tool for strategic planning. Management also uses the mission statement on a daily basis to help make decisions about the operation of the company.

The mission statement also plays a key role in evaluating how the employees deal with customers, with each other, and with vendors. For example, a long-term employee who managed the meat department at one of the Ukrop's stores refused to carry out the company's three-day expiration policy. He was warned the first time he was caught; the second time Mr. Ukrop fired him. When some people objected to the firing, Mr. Ukrop's response was "Considering our mission statement, how can we not do it?"

Managers at Ukrop's are not bound by as many policies as they used to be. Instead they are told to make decisions using common sense and the mission statement as guidelines. For instance, Ukrop's used to have a policy of not cashing any check over $400. But if a regular customer wants to cash a $500 check, they will cash it, because their mission statement demands superior customer service. The $400 figure is a guide, rather than a policy.

Ukrop's goes to great lengths in encouraging their employees to learn about the mission statement. For a while it was even printed on every grocery bag. Employees are encouraged to memorize the statement. Anyone who can recite the mission statement from memory gets a special pin and their name listed on the honor roll. Typically 50-70 people qualify each month. There are over 2,500 employees on the honor roll, out of a total of 5,000 employees.

Ukrop's works hard at recognizing their people. For example, at the annual picnic, those employees who have received letters of praise from customers are entered in the Parade of Champions. The promotion system is designed to enable the organization to have plenty of room for advancement, appropriate work titles, and financial levels. All of which speaks to the respect of the organization for its people.

Meetings at Ukrop's are usually started with some "mission in action" stories. These are stories about heroic things that employees do to carry out the mission. For example, stories about employees changing tires, delivering wedding cakes, and helping customers who have difficulties are common. According to Mr. Ukrop, these stories help people to understand the mission and to celebrate living it.

9.3   VCU Department of Psychology

Steve Robbins, Ph.D., Chair of the VCU Department of Psychology, is one of the best university level managers we have met. He led the development of the department's mission statement, based on Gast's laws, in 1994.

According to Prof. Robbins, the mission statement serves as the guide for the department. He refers to it for guidance on processes he wants implemented in the department. It creates a structure for the hiring process, and is used at the insistence of the other faculty as the basis for their strategic planning sessions. No faculty or staff hires are made unless the focus of the hiring (or new position) is consistent with the mission statement.

The mission statement sets a tone that the members of the department live their working lives by. Interestingly, when the department first created their mission statement, Prof. Robbins was not impressed with the part of the mission statement that listed the shared values. Instead, he was mainly interested in the part that listed the long range goals of the department. However, since then, he has discovered that the part of the mission statement that is used the most, the part that is most helpful, is the list of shared values. In Prof. Robbins's words,

> The values part serves as a basis for a sense of respect we are trying to instill in the faculty. We want people to feel safe to take risks and to be tolerant. We don't want people to feel that hard work is our goal, when actually our goal is excellence. Being held in high regard is not enough, we must be excellent. The mission statement represents the standards I will expect and will enforce, as long as I am Chair of the department.

Prof. Robbins uses the statement daily to frame decisions and to focus on values and goals. It serves as a cornerstone, especially when the department is under stress or changing circumstances. It gives continuity.

9.4 School of Allied Health Professions

The VCU/MCV School of Allied Health Professions developed a new mission statement, based on Gast's laws, early in 1995, under the leadership of Dean Thomas Barker, Ph.D.

Cecil Drain, Ph.D., the current Dean, has appointed one of his Chairs as the School Mission Manager. As a Chair, she attends all School Executive Committee meetings and reflects the decisions made against the school's mission statement. This has been an effective technique and has made the mission statement an important document in the decision making process. For example, some decisions most recently affected by this technique involve the structure of the Executive Committee meetings, the method and process for the evaluation of Chairs of all departments, and resolutions about the accountability of staff and faculty.

As another example, the mission statement was highlighted in the introduction of a recent report that Prof. Drain presented to the University President's Council. In the report he explained how the School positioned itself to earn top-10 nationwide rankings for five of its eight departments in 1998.

9.5 Coastal Hospice

Coastal Hospice, in Salisbury, MD, is a freestanding hospice that provides hospice and home health services for 4 counties on the eastern shore of

Maryland. Marion Keenan, President, led the effort to develop a new mission statement, based on Gast's laws, in 1992 (see Appendix K).

According to Ms. Keenan, the mission statement is an integral part of the daily work life. The mission statement is reproduced on the first page of the employee handbook. A large framed copy hangs in every room where decisions are made. According to Ms. Keenan, "you can't get away from it!".

Employees share the mission statement with every patient. Managers carefully review the statement with prospective employee and volunteer applicants to make sure they are willing to support the mission.

It is also used in daily decision making and in strategic planning, serving to constantly remind them what they are about. It has helped them to stabilize their direction in the face of the incredible changes that are occurring in the health care industry. As the organization ponders gut-wrenching changes, they ask themselves if the changes are consistent with their mission. If not, they consider other options. According to Ms. Keenan,

> Constant change makes it difficult to keep your footing because your footing is always changing. It would have been harder for me personally to not have a mission statement to work with. I may have been confused. A leader needs to be rooted in something important.

Ms. Keenan tells us that the Coastal Hospice staff literally lives the mission in their discussions and problem solving. People are not afraid to confront her on mission issues. For example, "You say one thing in the mission, but this decision speaks of another." The challenges are not one-upsmanship. They are based on serious concerns that help keep the staff on track. In her words,

> I believe in the mission statement as do most of my people. It is not hard to get the organization to live it. It inspires people, and they take it to heart. When I see how our people, one on one, work through tough problems, I know they believe it.

9.6 Bon Secours Health System

Dick O'Hallaron (the first author of this book) was CEO of St. Mary's Hospital in Richmond, VA from 1972–1987, and the regional vice-president for the Virginia area of the Bon Secours Health System from 1985–1987. The Sisters of Bon Secours organized an extremely successful health system, currently one of the largest Catholic health systems in the country, in 1983. At the same time they developed a mission statement for their new system (see Appendix L for their most recent version).

As CEO, Dick had a strong feeling that the mission statement was understood by most people and had a big impact on the day-to-day operation of the organization. The organization had a very caring environment. It held people in high esteem, including doctors, employees, volunteers and especially its patients. It had a special focus on high quality, whether it was keeping the hospital clean, serving good meals, or providing quality nursing and medical care. People were proud of the environment and liked working there. Bon Secures had an excellent mission statement, and the organization lived it. The mission statement was a powerful influence then, and it still is today.

The same mission statement was used by all 9 facilities in the early days of the Bon Secours health system, and thus provided continuity in culture across all the hospitals in the system. It was an important factor in the success of the organization, and triggered Dick's current passion for helping other organizations develop good mission statements.

The mission statement affected many parts of the organization. Dick used the mission statement extensively during orientation and routine training sessions for hospital employees and board members. In general, the organization used the mission statement as the basis for teaching employees how they should treat patients and each other.

The mission statement also served as the basic document for strategic planning, and Dick used it numerous times to help with major hirings and acquisitions. For example, he used it to screen applicants when he was hiring a CEO for the Great Britain province of the Bon Secours system.

He also used it to help rule out the purchase of a group of nursing homes in the US. The profitability of the prospective purchase was built on wage and benefit policies that did not fit the Bon Secours mission. What at first looked like a good investment wasn't, when one examined the employee benefits, which were practically nil. The company that owned the chain made their money by paying very low wages and offering practically no benefits.

In another case, the objective in the Bon Secours mission statement to care for the poor supported a system-wide policy of never refusing care to someone because they couldn't pay. It also helped influence a decision to open a satellite in Amelia County, one of the poorest and most underserved areas in Virginia. Bon Secours built a new health care center and staffed it with doctors, nurses, x-ray technicians, and lab people. The center took care of anyone who showed up, whether they could pay or not. The center won the Citation Award from the Catholic Hospital Association for outstanding works in the care of the poor. Eventually it became a self-sufficient enterprise and provides a continuing service to this day in an area that really needs it.

At one point the organization made the difficult decision to eliminate a certain job category in the pharmacy and lay off the 100 people that filled those jobs. Since the mission statement emphasized respect for people and a responsibility to provide productive employment, the board required Dick to make a report each month on the status of the people who had not been rehired yet. Each month, the board quietly extended the severance packages for the employees who were still unemployed but were actively trying to find jobs. At the end of a year, all but 2 out of 100 had found work, and no one had their severance package terminated before they were able to find work. Clearly, Bon Secours was an organization with an intuitive understanding of Gast's laws.

In the late 1980's Dick was chair of the finance committee of the Cincinnati based Sisters of Charity Health System. The members of this committee included a vice-president of the Federal Reserve, highly successful business people, academic people, members of religious orders, and hospital CEOs. An important purpose of the committee was to review the feasibility and financial impact of major programs proposed by member organizations of the system.

In many cases, the committee first reviewed the financial impact of the proposal, and then attempted to evaluate whether the proposal was consistent with the organization's mission statement. However, a number of committee members were uncomfortable with their level of understanding of the organization's mission.

To address this problem, Dick devised the following simple but effective technique, called a *mission reflection*, to help the board members learn about the mission of the organization. At the beginning of each finance committee meeting, one of the committee members would spend a few minutes describing what the mission meant to them. They might focus on some aspect of the mission, or they might describe how they felt the day's agenda related to the mission. The presentations were for the most part extemporaneous and informal. It was inspiring to hear each person's feeling about the mission of the organization and what it meant to the individually personally. After about 18 months of this practice, everyone clearly understood what the mission was all about, but the committee chose to continue the practice anyway because they valued the comments.

Some of the finance committee members liked the idea of mission reflections so much that they began doing it with other committees and boards that they served with. Over a period of several years, without any directive or mandate from anyone, the practice of mission reflections spread throughout the board level committees of the system and its numerous hospitals. The practice eventually spread outside of the Sisters of Charity system. One of the board members of their Denver hospital, a major stockholder of a multinational corporation, instituted the practice of mission reflections at the board meetings of his own organization.

Concluding remarks

These are just a few examples that illustrate how different organizations, large and small, for-profit and non-profit, are using their mission statements in the day-to-day operations of their businesses. From these examples, we can draw a few conclusions about effective mission statements.

First, and most important, the head of the organization believes in the mission statement completely and recognizes it as an important tool. Depending on the type of organization (i.e., corporation, section, or department) this person might be the chairman, president, or department head. Without support from the top, a mission statement is not worth the paper it is printed on, and none of the techniques we have taught you will make any difference.

Second, the most effective mission statements address all of Gast's laws.

Third, the mission statement is used on a daily basis and plays a significant role in the operation of the business. It is used in strategic planning, in problem solving, in day-to-day decision making, and in promoting the objectives of the organization.

Finally, the mission is well distributed and visible. Managers, employees, vendors, contractors, and customers know about the mission statement and understand it.

Many successful organizations use their mission statement as a powerful management tool. If you follow our advice and base your mission statement on Gast's laws, you too can create an effective mission statement. Good luck!

Appendix A

The Four Steps to an Effective Mission Statement

1. Organize a mission team.

2. Use Gast's laws to construct the fundamental objectives of the organization.

3. Use the fundamental objectives to construct the mission statement.

4. Use the mission statement regularly and strategically.

Appendix B

Gast's Laws

A business must:

1. Produce a want-satisfying commodity or service, and continually improve its ability to meet needs.

2. Increase the wealth or quality of life of society through the economic use of labor and capital.

3. Provide opportunities for the productive employment of people.

4. Provide opportunities for the satisfaction of normal occupational desires.

5. Provide just wages for labor.

6. Provide a just return on capital.

Appendix C

The Baldrige Award Winners

1998. Boeing Airlift and Tanker Programs, Solar Turbines Inc., Texas Nameplate Conpany Inc.

1997. Merrill Lynch Credit, Xerox Business Services, 3M Dental Products Division, Solectron.

1996. ADAC Laboratories, Custom Research, Dana Commercial Credit, Trident Precision Manufacturing.

1995. Armstrong World Industries Building Products Operations, Corning Telecommunications Products Division.

1994. AT&T Consumer Communications Services, GTE Directories Corporation, Wainwright Industries.

1993. Ames Rubber, Eastman Chemical Company.

1992. AT&T Network Systems Group Transmission Systems Business Unit, AT&T Universal Card Services, Granite Rock Company, Texas Instruments, Defense Systems & Electronics Group.

1991. Marlow Industries, Solectron, Zytec.

1990. Cadillac Motor Car Company, Federal Express, IBM Rochester AS/400 Division, Wallace Company.

1989. Milliken & Company, Xerox Business Products & Systems.

1988. Globe Metalurgical, Motorola, Westinghouse Electric Commercial Nuclear Fuel Division.

Appendix D

Anheuser-Busch Technology Acquisition Team

Mission Statement

Vision

The Technology Acquisition Team supports the mission of Anheuser-Busch Companies, Inc. and the Management Systems Group. Our aim is to provide key procurement services to Anheuser-Busch Companies, Inc. and its affiliates for all information technologies. These services include negotiation, risk management, vendor/product selection expertise, leadership in knowledge of industry trends, and other activities that promote the success of our customers. Our commitment in providing our services is to be *the best* — efficient, effective, and constantly improving our ability to meet or exceed our customers' expectations.

We will ensure a quality return on the investment our company has made in our team, by striving to add value, eliminate waste and achieve the lowest total system cost for our customers. Our contribution to the quality of life is to promote the organization's responsibilities for our impact on the environment and society.

We will do our best to respect our vendors and their investments of time and resources. We will treat them fairly and honestly in striving to award our business based on excellent service, superior quality and competitive price. We intend to build long term relationships with the best suppliers in the industry.

Values

In working together to achieve our vision, the people of the Technology Acquisition Team are guided by a set of shared beliefs that make progress possible. Our task is to strive for constant improvement in making these beliefs a reality:

TRUST. We believe in:

- A trust among team members that holds each member accountable.

- Earning trust by recognizing the appropriate priority of our customers' needs while protecting the interests of the company and our customers.

PEOPLE. We believe in:

- The fundamental respect and dignity for each individual with whom we have contact in the pursuit of our vision.

- Recognizing the contributions of our team members and providing them with opportunities for satisfying and financially rewarding work with continuous opportunities for personal development and advancement.

- Our team's ability to be open to new ideas and our collective effectiveness to anticipate future technological and service needs of our customers.

QUALITY. We believe in:

- A fundamental commitment to continuous improvement of our services, targeted to ultimately achieve customer delight.

- Providing our customers with the highest ideals of timeliness, accuracy, consistency, and completeness in our work.

Appendix E

British Airways

Mission Statement

British Airways mission is to be the undisputed leader in world travel. Our values are to be:

- Safe and secure

- Honest and responsible

- Innovative and team-spirited

- Global and a caring good neighbor

Our goals are:

- To be the customers first choice.

- We want British Airways to be the air line of first choice in our key markets.

- We want inspired teams of people building and benefiting from the company's success, sharing a cause, feeling good about working together and delighting the customer.

- To enjoy strong profitability.

- We need to meet investors expectations and secure the future.

- To be truly global.

- With a global network and a global outlook, we want to be recognized everywhere for superior value in world travel.

Appendix F

Ford Motor Company

Mission, Values, and Guiding Principles

Mission

Ford Motor Company is a worldwide leader in automotive-related products and services as well as in newer industries such as aerospace, communications, and financial services. Our mission is to improve continually our products and services to meet our customers' needs, allowing us to prosper as a business and to provide a reasonable return for our stockholders, the owners of our business.

Values

How we accomplish our mission is as important as the mission itself. Fundamental to success for the company are these basic values:

- People — Our people are the source of our strength. They provide our corporate intelligence and determine our reputation and vitality. Involvement and teamwork are our core human values.

- Products — Our products are the end result of our efforts, and they should be the best in serving customers worldwide. As our products are viewed, so are we viewed.

93

- Profits — Profits are the ultimate measure of how efficiently we provide customers with the best products for their needs. Profits are required to survive and grow.

Guiding Principles

- Quality comes first. To achieve customer satisfaction, the quality of our products and services must be our number one priority.

- Customers are the focus of everything we do. Our work must be done with our customers in mind, providing better products and services than our competition.

- Continuous improvement is essential to our success. We must strive for excellence in everything we do, in our products, in their safety and value, and in our services, our human relations, our competitiveness, and our profitability.

- Employee involvement is our way of life. We are a team. We must treat each other with trust and respect.

- Dealers and suppliers are our partners. The company must maintain mutually beneficial relationships with dealers, suppliers, and our other business associates.

- Integrity is never compromised. The conduct of our company worldwide must be pursued in a manner that is socially responsible and commands respect for its integrity and for its positive contributions to society. Our doors are open to men and women alike without discrimination and without regard to ethnic origin or personal beliefs.

Appendix G

Johnson & Johnson

Our Credo

We believe our first responsibility is to the doctor, nurses and patients,
to mothers and all others who use our products and services.
In meeting their needs everything we do must be of high quality.
We must constantly strive to reduce our costs
in order to maintain reasonable prices.
Customers' orders must be serviced promptly and accurately.
Our suppliers and distributors must have an opportunity
to make a fair profit.

We are responsible to our employees,
the men and women who work with us throughout the world.
Everyone must be considered as an individual.
We must respect their dignity and recognize their merit.
They must have a sense of security in their jobs.
Compensation must be fair and adequate,
and working conditions clean, orderly and safe.
We must be mindful of ways to help our employees fulfill
their family responsibilities.
Employees must feel free to make suggestions and complaints.
There must be equal opportunity for employment, development
and advancement for those qualified.
We must provide competent management,

and their actions must be just and ethical.

We are responsible to the communities in which we live and work
and to the world community as well.
We must be good citizens - support good works and charities
and bear our fair share of taxes.
We must encourage civic improvements and better health and education.
We must maintain in good order
the property we are privileged to use,
protecting the environment and natural resources.

Our final responsibility is to our stockholders.
Business must make a sound profit.
We must experiment with new ideas.
Research must be carried on, innovative programs developed
and mistakes paid for.
New equipment must be purchased, new facilities provided
and new products launched.
Reserves must be created to provide for adverse times.
When we operate according to these principles,
the stockholders should realize a fair return.

Appendix H

Ukrop's

Vision, Mission, and Shared Values

Vision

The vision of Ukrop's is to be a world-class provider of food and services.

Mission

The mission of Ukrop's is to serve our customers and community efficiently and effectively while treating our customers, associates, and suppliers as we personally like to be treated. We will achieve profitable growth and long-term financial success while promoting an atmosphere of mutual trust, honesty and integrity.

Shared Values

We believe we can best fulfill our vision and accomplish our mission by living these values daily:

- Superior Customer Service — resulting from great execution, a caring attitude, and a sense of urgency.

- Honesty and Fairness — acting openly, equitably and consistently in all we do.

- Superior Quality and Freshness — uncompromising in our commitment.

- Cost Consciousness — minimizing waste and vigorously pursuing continuous improvement, resulting in lower prices and greater values.

- Teamwork — coming together as a diverse workforce to achieve our shared vision.

- Atmosphere — fostering an environment that is safe, clean, challenging, and fun.

- Health and Fitness — strengthening our bodies for productive and creative minds.

- Competence — performing our jobs effectively and being informed and excited about our food and services.

- Lifelong Learning — seeking knowledge and enthusiastically sharing it with others

- Quality of Life — committing to improving the lives of our families and well-being of our community

Appendix I

VCU Department of Psychology

Mission Statement

Vision

The Department of Psychology is a national leader promoting the understanding of behavior through the integration of scholarly inquiry, teaching, and service. We promote an environment conducive to learning, with a special emphasis on applied societally relevant psychology.

We lead the way in improving the quality of life in society through the development of knowledge and technology, finding ways of addressing human problems, and educating people to be responsible citizens and effective leaders.

We achieve excellence by continually measuring our performance and productivity as scholars, teachers, contributors to society, and as a Department, in order to effectively meet the changing needs of our customers, whether they be students, staff, faculty, the Commonwealth of Virginia, or society.

We are committed to create and enhance mechanisms for the recognition of people's work, and to provide access to growth and advancement for faculty, staff, and students. We advocate fair compensation, and see creative means of developing and managing compensations for our people and Department.

In all endeavors, we strive to use resources cost-effectively so that we can best achieve this mission and the missions of the college of Humanities and Sciences and of Virginia Commonwealth University.

Values

Our work is created with excellence, conceived in wisdom, and aimed at improving the quality of life. Our productivity is maintained in an environment of fairness, mutual respect, and enjoyment.

How we accomplish our mission is as important as the mission itself. Fundamental to the success of the Department are these basic values:

- Mutual Respect — We value and refuse to devalue other people, including our faculty, staff, students, members of our University community, and all other constituents.

- Enjoyment — We strive to create an environment that we look forward to entering each day.

- Wisdom — We apply our knowledge and expertise with compassion and caring.

- Fairness — We treat others as we like to be treated, with trust and respect. We maintain clearly and equitable access to resources in the Department for faculty, staff, and students.

- Excellence — Creatively doing whatever we must and whatever we aim for, with an intent to improve continually, so we can affect others and be proud of what we have done.

- Improved Quality of Life — In order to make our increasingly diverse society better, we contribute knowledge, educate people, and work to solve human problems.

- Productivity — Teamwork and individual efforts are both parts of a productive environment. we value and support our own work and the work of others.

Appendix J

School of Allied Health Professions

MISSION

The School of Allied Health Professions serves as an international leader in the education of excellent, innovative, and responsible allied health professionals. Educational formats that are technologically advanced and accessible to students through on-campus and distance learning are emphasized. In addition, the School, responsive to the needs of society, promotes excellence in health care service, and encourages collaborative research that generates state-of-the-art and specialized knowledge.

The School is an integral part of Virginia Commonwealth University and its Medical College of Virginia Campus. The School recognizes the importance of being accountable to the students and their families, the Commonwealth, faculty, staff, alumni, and other benefactors by using resources effectively. Strong linkages with clinical educators, preceptors, and the community are essential to the success of the School.

The School fosters fair and equitable work responsibilities and compensation to faculty and staff. It nurtures continuous growth in their knowledge base and productivity. The School furnishes an accessible, secure, and pleasant physical setting that enhances the cohesion, interaction, and morale of the students, faculty, and staff.

The School serves and represents its member departments. It is organized in a decentralized structure that empowers the departments to achieve leadership in each of their respective disciplines. The School derives its strength from professional diversity that is based upon cooperative interdisciplinary education, research, and service.

In pursuit of this vision, the School emphasizes the following values:

- Accountability — We take responsibility for our attitudes, actions, and judgements.

- Cooperation — We collaborate through the practice of open communication, trust, and respect.

- Dignity of the Individual — We respect the value and uniqueness of each individual.

- Enjoyment — We value internal well-being, creative enrichment, and a spirit of joyfulness.

- Excellence — We practice and promote the highest standard of quality performance and care of the individual.

- Fulfillment of Potential — We facilitate continual professional development and personal growth.

- Innovation — We encourage and support creativity.

- Integrity — We conduct ourselves in a forthright and honorable manner as demonstrated by actions that are hones and trustworthy.

Appendix K

Coastal Hospice

OUR MISSION

Coastal Hospice is a health care organization dedicated to preserving the dignity and quality of life. We offer both comprehensive hospice care for the terminally ill and selected home health services to residents of Maryland's lower Eastern Shore. In addition to providing physical care, we promote the emotional and spiritual growth of patients, enabling them to live their lives to the fullest. Our mission includes education in the care of the terminally ill and support to the bereaved.

As responsible stewards we will use our resources effectively and productively, conscientiously preserving our assets. We will continually improve Coastal Hospice in order to meet our community's changing needs with the highest quality, cost effective services. We will strive to exceed requirements for licensure, accreditation and other recognized professional standards.

We encourage pursuit of our ideals, professional development and teamwork. We value our associates and respect the service given to patients by staff, volunteers, attending physicians and all others who support Coastal Hospice.

OUR VALUES

- AFFIRMING LIFE. We believe that human life has inherent dignity and is worthy of celebration. We hope our patients will live life to its fullest. Coastal Hospice will neither hasten nor unduly postpone death for those who are terminally ill. We will strive to alleviate pain, to provide physical comfort, to encourage emotional and spiritual growth, to foster reconciliation, and to enhance each patient's relationship with others.

- RESPECT. We respect the dignity of all who serve and are served by Coastal Hospice. We honor each patient's privacy and right to make decisions concerning treatment. We encourage each colleague's professional development. We will foster a work environment characterized by effective teamwork, clear direction and recognition of individual contributions.

- COMPASSION. We will respond promptly with our presence to patients and families needing assurance, guidance, and relief from suffering. We encourage caring support, comfort, communication, understanding, empathy and listening.

- TRUST. Trust is the bond which holds a community together; open and honest communication is essential for our work. Our patients and families have unique responsibilities and capabilities for providing care and we trust them to make good decisions. Reciprocally, we hope to deserve their trust and that of our community.

- COMMITMENT. We are committed to the highest standards of care and recognize that personal relationship with each patient this requires. We pledge to provide care regardless of a patient's ability to pay. We will lead in educating others about hospice and home care. We will fulfill our responsibilities to staff, volunteers, attending physicians, colleagues in health care, clergy, supporters, media, and the community at large.

- QUALITY. We will improve the quality of our services continually. Each associate is a partner in fostering Coastal Hospice's growth and development and is empowered to respond caringly to our patients and their families.

Appendix L

Bon Secours Health System

MISSION

Recognizing the dignity of all persons, we provide compassionate health care services contributing to the physical, social, emotional, and spiritual well-being of those we serve. We commit ourselves to help bring people to wholeness by:

- understanding and responding to health care needs (especially unmet needs).

- developing the potential of those who serve with us.

- advocating a just and equitable public health policy.

- modeling justice in the workplace.

Guided by our values and our responsibility to the communities we serve, we will achieve planned growth in response to community need, while continually improving our systems and services so as to become ever more faithful to our Mission.

VALUES

- **Respect.** We treat all people well because we believe each person has dignity.

105

- **Justice.** We support, protect and promote the rights of all individuals and have special concern for the poor.

- **Integrity.** We are honest in our dealings; our behavior is consistent with our thoughts, feelings and values.

- **Stewardship.** We use all of Bon Secours resources in a responsible way.

- **Innovation.** We look for new ways to meet people's needs and improve our service.

- **Compassion.** We experience and express empathy with the life situations of others.

- **Quality.** We continuously improve our service through understanding and acting on the needs and expectations of being served.

- **Growth.** We strive to expand our services to meet new needs, and we promote the development of our co-workers.

Appendix M

Examples of Organizational Values

Here are some examples of organization values and their descriptions that you can use as a point of departure when you write your mission statement. They are included to help you understand what we mean by the notion of an organizational value. Use these as starting points only; always write your mission statement in your own words so that it describes the unique nature of your organization.

Accountability: Individual faculty, staff, and students are accountable to each other, the department Chair, the school, the university, and the larger society.

Accountability: We take responsibility for our attitudes, actions, and judgments.

Affirming life: We believe that human life has inherent dignity and is worthy of celebration. We hope our patients will live life to its fullest. Coastal Hospice will neither hasten nor unduly postpone death for those who are terminally ill. We will strive to alleviate pain, to provide physical comfort, to encourage emotional and spiritual growth, to foster reconciliation, and to enhance each patient's relationship with others.

Ambition: We encourage our people to be ambitious in their pursuit of knowledge, and work toward advancement within the organization.

Anticipation: Anticipation of, and planning for the future health care needs of our service area, is important to our constituents.

Appreciation for resources: Company assets and financial resources are investments in our future and receive our utmost respect.

Atmosphere: We will work to create an atmosphere within this plant that is safe, clean, challenging, and fun.

Attentiveness: We attend to the medical needs of the families of our active duty members, our retirees and their families, whenever we are able, for just as the family supports the force, so must we support the family.

Bravery: We admire those in our organization who have demonstrated bravery in the pursuit of their rescue efforts.

Caring: We care for all persons as unique human beings worthy of our courtesy, compassion and respect.

Caring: We will always have a caring and responsive attitude toward patients, their families and guests.

Choices: We pursue the highest ethical standards in our decisions and in our actions.

Christian identity: The Christian Identity of our work is paramount to the motivation of our mission.

Citizenship: We will support civic activities to improve the quality of life for our fellow man.

Collaboration: We work together in a spirit of teamwork to serve others.

Commitment: We are committed to the highest standards of care and recognize the personal relationship with each patient this requires. We pledge to provide care regardless of a patient's ability to pay. We will lead in educating others about hospice and home care. We will fulfill our responsibilities to staff, volunteers, attending physicians, colleagues in health care, clergy, supporters, media, and the community at large.

Communication: We will promote honest, current and continuous two-way communication throughout the organization.

Compassion: We will respond promptly with our presence to patients and families needing assurance, guidance, and relief from suffering. We encourage caring support, comfort, communication, understanding, empathy and listening.

Compassion: We enhance the dignity of all people by demonstrating care and respect.

Competence: We pursue excellence in our healing efforts.

Consistency: We will encourage a consistent level of excellent service to all our constituents.

Continuous improvement: We will promote continuous improvement in the quality of the work of faculty, staff, students, and alumni.

Continuous improvement: Continuous improvement is essential to our success. We must strive for excellence in everything we do: in our products, in their safety and value–and in our services, our human relations, our competitiveness, and our profitability.

Continuous improvement: We will continuously improve in all aspects of our enterprise.

Contribution: We empower each person to fully use gifts and talents, and hold each other accountable to the fullest extent.

Cooperation: We collaborate through the practice of open communication, trust, and respect.

Cost consciousness: We will minimize waste and vigorously pursue productivity improvements

Creativity: We seek the best way to serve and to use the resources entrusted to us.

Customers: Customers are the focus of everything we do–Our work must be done with our customers in mind, providing better products and services than our competition.

Dealers and suppliers as partners: The Company must maintain mutually beneficial relationships with dealers, suppliers, and our other business associates.

Dependability: We will be known as dependable dedicated providers of service to all our constituents.

Development: The development of each of our associates is key to the success of our customer service mission.

Dignity of the individual: We respect the value and uniqueness of each individual.

Diligence: We will be diligent in our effort to provide high quality at all times.

Diversity: Diversity is a strength upon which this organization is built.

Efficiency: We will be efficient in the use of our resources.

Employee involvement: Employee involvement is our way of life– We are a team, and we must treat each other with trust and respect.

Enjoyment: We strive to create an environment that we look forward to entering each day.

Enjoyment: We value internal well being, creative enrichment, and a spirit of joyfulness.

Ethical conduct: Ethical conduct is a way of life expected by all who work with our organization.

Excellence: We practice and promote the highest standard of quality performance and care of the individual.

Excellence: Superior quality in every task is our minimum standard.

Fair Return: We will provide a fair return to participants and support organizations.

Fairness: We treat others as we like to be treated, with trust and respect. We maintain clearly defined and equitable access to resources in the Department for faculty, staff, and students.

Fairness: We believe in fairness in matters of compensation, benefits, promotion and tenure, scheduling, grading, resource allocation, and handling disputes.

Faithfulness: We will be faithful to the commitment we have made for excellence in the provision of services and products.

Fulfillment of potential: We facilitate continual professional development and personal growth.

Growth and application of continuous quality improvement: Provide help and seek to influence business, educational and governmental entities in pursuit of continuous quality improvement.

Growth and development of people: Create an environment where in individuals may grow through a process of reciprocal sharing of knowledge and experience.

Health and fitness: Essential for productive and creative minds.

Honesty and fairness: Treating others as we personally would like to be treated.

Honesty and integrity: All business is conducted in a forthright and trustworthy manner.

Improved quality of life: In order to make our increasingly diverse society better, we contribute knowledge, educate people, and work to solve human problems.

Improvement: We will improve the quality of life and respond to opportunities to improve the economic viability of the community.

Innovation: Innovation is the rule, not the exception. Creative and constructive ideas are sought from all employees.

Innovation: We will identify opportunities arising from new human needs and new professional technologies and promptly assemble the talent and resources to exploit these opportunities. Our innovative capability is one of the foundations upon which our leadership capacity is built.

Innovation: We encourage and support creativity.

Integrity: Integrity is never compromised — The conduct of our Company worldwide must be pursued in a manner that is socially responsible and commands respect for its integrity and for its positive contributions to society. Our doors are open to men and women like without discrimination and without regard to ethnic origin or personal beliefs.

Integrity: We conduct ourselves in a forthright and honorable manner as demonstrated by actions that are honest and trust worthy.

Justice: We will be just in our decisions and rewards.

Kindness: Kindness is a quality we look for in all our associates.

Leadership: We believe in leadership through excellence and will establish new directions by talent and example, influencing the behavior of other institutions.

Learning: We will build on our heritage of the Carnegie Plan and become the leading institution that combines first rate research with outstanding undergraduate education through our focus on learning and problem solving.

Life-long learning: Life long learning is necessary for personal and career growth.

Long-term profitability and growth: This is a measure of success which associates share through bonuses and new opportunities.

Loyalty: Loyalty is shared. The individual is true to the organization and the organization is true to each person.

Mutual respect: We value and refuse to devalue other people, including our staff, faculty, students, members of our University community, and all other constituents.

People: Our people are the source of our strength. They provide our corporate intelligence and determine our reputation and vitality. Involvement and teamwork are our core human values.

People: We believe in the fundamental respect and dignity for each individual with whom we have contact in the pursuit of our vision. Recognizing the contributions of our team members and providing them with opportunities for satisfying and financially rewarding work with continuous opportunities for personal development and advancement. Our team's ability to be open to new paradigms and our collective effectiveness to anticipate future technological and service needs of our customers.

People: People are our greatest asset. We could not function without our people; they are the keys to our organization's success.

Personal development: Personal development is the foundation of our long-term ability to serve our customers well.

Productivity: Teamwork and individual efforts are both parts of a productive environment. We value and support our own work and the work of others.

Products: Our products are the end result of our efforts, and they should be the best in serving customers world wide. As our products are viewed, so are we viewed.

Profits: Profits are the ultimate measure of how efficiently we provide customers with the best products for their needs. Profits are required to survive and grow.

Quality: We will improve the quality of our services continually.

Quality: We believe in a fundamental commitment to continuous improvement of our services, targeted to ultimately achieve customer delight.

Providing our customers with the highest ideals of timeliness, accuracy, consistency and completeness in our work.

Quality: We will focus our energies on understanding the needs of the communities we serve while applying Quality principles to continuously improve our efforts in fulfilling these needs.

Quality of life: The quality of work life within this organization is a key factor.

Quality service: Our quality of service is consistently high.

Reliability: Reliability is the trademark of our service.

Respect: We respect the dignity of all who serve and are served by Coastal Hospice. We honor each patient's privacy and right to make decisions concerning treatment. We encourage each colleague's professional development. We will foster a work environment characterized by effective teamwork, clear direction and recognition of individual contributions.

Respect: We foster great respect for the dignity of each individual including our employees, volunteers and medical staff and their individual commitment and contributions.

Respect for the individual: People are our most important asset. We strive to treat one another with dignity, respect and as a vital part of our organization.

Responsibility: We recognize the responsibility each of us has for our own actions.

Responsiveness: We will make every effort to be responsive to the needs of our students, faculty and employees.

Risk taking: We respect those in the organization who are innovative thoughtful risk takers.

Safety: Safety is one of our highest priorities to protect our employees and customers.

Service to our customers: Our customers are the only reason for our business. Meeting their needs is our most important concern.

Stability: We will aggressively work to provide stability and security to our staff.

Staff development: The development of our staff is the key to excellence.

Stewardship: We will be good stewards of the resources entrusted to our use.

Superior customer service: The result of great execution, a caring attitude, and a sense of urgency.

Superior customer service: Our purpose is to delight our customer.

Support: We support the combat readiness of the Navy and Marine Corps.

Teamwork: Where leadership and cooperation come together.

Teamwork: Teamwork binds us together. Pride in our accomplishments comes from cooperation among students, faculty, staff, and alumni.

Transcending disciplinary boundaries: We are a seamless university without traditional departmental boundaries.

Transfer to Society: We affirm our responsibility to serve society through the transfer of technology, continuing education programs, public service and enrichment of the community through the arts.

Trust: Trust is the bond which holds a community together; open and honest communication is essential for our work. Our patients and families have unique responsibilities and capabilities for providing care and we trust them to make good decisions. Reciprocally, we hope to deserve their trust and that of our community.

Trust: We believe in a trust among team members that holds each member accountable. Earning trust by recognizing the appropriate priority of our customer's needs while protecting the interest of the company and our customers.

Truth: Being truthful to our constituents is a value we never compromise.

Understanding: Trying to understand the problems of our constituents is the only way we will learn to build solutions to their problems.

Value: The best combination of price and quality.

Value oriented management: We seek value-added contributions from our managers and associates.

We care: We care for each other just as we care for our patients. This is the basis of the teamwork and trust that must exist for us to succeed.

Wisdom: We apply our knowledge and expertise with compassion and caring.

Witness to Gospel values: The Gospel values are an essential part of our mission.

Appendix N

The Group Interview

The *group interview* is a powerful and general way for a workshop or work group leader to get a group's opinion on a collection of interview questions. In the context of developing mission statements, we use the group interview as a way to ask newly formed mission teams various questions about mission statements in general, their existing mission statements, and their feelings about developing a new mission statement. Section 6.2 gives examples of some of the questions we like to ask. However, in this section, we will describe the group interview in a general workshop or work group context.

The basic idea behind the group interview is to provide a structured way for group members to pair up and ask each other questions. Having the group members ask themselves the questions in this way has a number of benefits:

1. *Active involvement:* All participants are actively involved, reporting answers and asking questions. No one is able simply to sit back and listen. Everyone talking at once creates excitement and energy.

2. *Anonymity:* All answers are recorded anonymously so that each person's opinions will be given equal consideration regardless of his or her role or position in the organization. It levels hierarchy and mixes "in groups" and "out groups." It is very effective with mixed groups (professional-lay, provider-consumer, adult-juvenile, etc.).

3. *Candor:* When people talk in pairs, they tend to be more open and honest. In larger groups they become overly concerned about what

others think. Peer pressure and superiority cannot operate.

4. *Informality:* Participants have the opportunity to meet and talk privately with their colleagues, some of whom they may not have known. The exercise helps people get to know one another around a substantive exchange, rather than just names and positions.

5. *Objectivity:* The interviewer can only ask clarifying questions about his or her opinions and is not permitted to argue or contend responses. Likewise, the spokespersons in the group summaries are not allowed to let their own opinions influence their reporting. Thus, the design seeks objectivity as it casts the participants in the role of social scientists gathering data.

6. *Involvement in analysis:* Instead of outside experts analyzing data, participants experience the difficulty of consolidating the data to a few key points and must confront the diversity of viewpoints.

7. *Exposure to ideas:* Participants ask questions, listen to responses rather than argue, ask more questions to fully understand answers, and when the data is fed back, become exposed to the opinions, perceptions, and concerns of their peers. This enables them to relate their own ideas to those of their co-workers.

STEP 1: Develop the questions

The questions are usually developed beforehand, either from prior interviews with prospective participants or by workshop planners, to elicit information on questions of relevance to the goals of the workshop. A good interview question would require some thought and reflection and direct the respondent to organize their experience into some useful categories. It is often helpful to ask for a specific number of ideas. Here are the types of workshop questions that might be posed.

1. Can you identify two or three ways in which your relationships with your superiors are similar to how you, in turn, relate to your subordinates? Can you identify several differences?

2. What are the three greatest barriers you face in your organization in getting one of your ideas accepted and implemented?

3. What are your goals and expectations for the workshop? What may inhibit you in achieving these goals?

4. What do you feel will be the greatest changes in your field in the next twenty years?

As the questions illustrate, they can cover substantive ideas (4), workshop goals (3), management issues (1), or change issues (2). One concern should be to develop a set of questions of similar complexity so that they can be answered in the 3–5 minutes allotted. The set should explore different issues.

Experience has shown that 6 – 12 questions is appropriate, so that interviewing and reporting do not take too much time (1 1/2–2 hours). It is always helpful to have a few more questions than you plan to use, in case there are more participants than anticipated. However, as described in Step 3, the number you use depends on the size of the group.

STEP 2: Prepare the interview sheet

To prepare for the workshop, each question should be typed at the top of an *interview sheet*. One complete set of questions should be made for each *interview line*. The notion of an interview line is explained next in Step 3.

STEP 3: Design and run the group interview

A. Configure the interview lines

In a group interview, pairs of people sit across from each other at one or more tables. Each person is called an *interviewer*. The group of interviewers sitting on one side of a table is called an *interview line*. Each table has two lines. One line is designated the *stationary line* and the other line is designated the *moving line* (more on these in Step 3-C).

For example, suppose we have 20 interviewers sitting at 2 tables, with 5 per table side. Then we would say that we have 4 interview lines, each of size 5. On the other hand, if the 20 interviewers were sitting at one table, with 10 per side, then we would say we have 2 interview lines, each of size 10.

The most difficult aspect of designing a group interview is matching the number of questions with the number and size of the interview lines. For groups divisible by 4, it is easy, as illustrated below:

Group size	No. and size of interview line	No. of questions
20	2 lines of 10	10
20	4 lines of 5	5
24	4 lines of 6	6
24	2 lines of 12	12
28	4 lines of 7	7
32	4 lines of 8	8
36	4 lines of 9	9

If you have an uneven number of group members, you can have each each extra group member double up with an interviewer on one the stationary lines.

It is important to have the full group in attendance before starting. Sometimes it is useful to begin with some other short activity — such as workshop goal-setting — to wait until all are there. It is a powerful beginning because once under way, people are involved in the interview until it is finished.

B. Distribute the question sheets

After the interview lines are formed and the interviewers are seated in their interview lines, pass out the question sheets, one per person so that each interview line has a full set of questions. Each interviewer gets exactly one question. The order that questions are handed out is not important.

C. Conduct the group interview

At this point you are ready to conduct the group interview:

1. Each interviewer should have exactly one question, and each interview line should have a full set of questions.

2. The next step is to start the group interviews. The interviewers in each stationary line should ask the person seated directly across from them the question on their interview sheet. Each person who is asked a question has about 1–2 minutes to answer the question. The person who asks the questions should write down a brief summary of the reply on their question sheet.

3. Next, repeat the process, with the people on the moving line asking the questions of their partners on the stationary line.

4. After about 5 minutes, the group leader should call everyone to attention, and then ask the people in each moving line to stand up with their question sheet in hand, and rotate one chair to their left.

5. Repeat steps 2 – 5 until the original partners are again facing each other across the table. At this point, the interviews are finished.

STEP 4: Analyze the data

After the group interview in Step 3 is finished, assemble an analysis team for each question. The analysis team for a particular question consists of all the interviewers who were responsible for asking that question. For example, if the group interview had five questions, then all the people responsible for asking the first question would gather in some part of the room. Similarly for the other four questions.

Each analysis team should select a team leader and a recorder. Each team should then produce a brief written report that summarizes all the responses to their team's question. The idea is to identify and summarize the key themes in the responses. Do not, under any circumstances, identify the source or sources of any responses. Responses must be anonymous for the group interview to work.

STEP 5: Report

When the analysis teams have finished, reassemble the entire group. The team leaders for each analysis team gives a brief report (2–3 minutes) on the findings of the team. Questions and comments can be taken after each report.

The workshop leader should make arrangements to have the reports from the analysis team written up so that there is a record of the reports and so that follow up can be encouraged. Be sure to thank everyone involved, and then close the group interview.

Appendix O

About the Authors

RICHARD O'HALLARON

Richard O'Hallaron is a former Affiliate Professor at the Medical College of VA, Virginia Commonwealth University, Richmond, VA. He has also served on the faculty at Washington University in St. Louis, Missouri. He is a Life Fellow in the American College of Healthcare Executives, as well as a Life Fellow in the American Academy of Healthcare Administrators.

Richard received his BS and MHA from St. Louis University in St. Louis, Missouri. Since 1958 he has published over 30 articles in local, national and international publications focusing on a range of subjects such as ethics, marketing, quality improvement and organizational mission. He has served on local, national and international boards, and has been recognized for a number of innovative achievements. He spent 30 years as a senior healthcare executive, serving as an assistant, associate, CEO, regional vice president, and system vice president of development, before retiring in 1988. Since then he has taught business management and strategic planning at MCV. He also runs a consulting business called Mission Incorporated, which focuses on helping organizations articulate their mission and values, as well as managing these issues. Richard has lectured throughout the U.S., the Far East, and Great Britain, with a particular interest in and recognized as an expert on the subject of organizational mission and values. Richard his wife Phyllis have seven children and have been married for 45 years. For more information, please see www.erols.com/rdoh.

DAVID O'HALLARON

David O'Hallaron is an Associate Professor of Computer Science and Electrical and Computer Engineering at Carnegie Mellon University, Pittsburgh, PA.

While at Carnegie Mellon, David has lead groups that developed the iWarp parallel computer system with Intel and the Fx parallelizing compiler. He currently leads a group that is using parallel computer systems to model the ground motion of the LA basin during strong earthquakes. In 1997, his first Ph.D. student won the CMU School of Computer Science Distinguished Dissertation Award. In 1998 he was awarded the Alan Newell Award for Research Excellence by the Carnegie Mellon School of Computer Science for his work with the Quake project. David has published over 40 research articles, edited volumes for Springer-Verlag and IOSPress, and coauthored a 1998 book about the iWarp project for MIT Press. David, his wife Helen, and four sons live in Pittsburgh, PA. For more information, please see www.cs.cmu.edu/~droh.

Bibliography

[1] ABRAHMS, J. *The Mission Statement Book: 301 Corporate Mission Statements from America's Top Companies.* 10 Speed Press, Berkeley, CA, 1995.

[2] CAMPBELL, A. What is business for? *Strategic Planning Society News* (November 1988).

[3] CAMPBELL, A., DEVINE, M., AND YOUNG, D. *A Sense of Mission.* Hutchinson Business Books Limited, London, England, 1990.

[4] CAMPBELL, A., AND NASH, L. L. *A Sense of Mission.* Addison-Wesley, Reading, MA, 1992.

[5] CAMPBELL, A., AND TAWADEY, K. *Mission and Business Philosophy.* Butterworth-Heinemann Ltd., Oxford, England, 1992.

[6] CAMPBELL, A., AND YEUNG, S. Missionaries of the corporate culture. *Management Consultancy* (November 1990), 46–47.

[7] COLLINS, J. C., AND PORRAS, J. I. *Built to Last, Successful Habits of Visionary Companies.* HarperCollins, New York, NY, 97.

[8] COVEY, S. R. *The 7 Habits of Highly Effective People.* Simon & Schuster, New York, NY, 1990.

[9] DENISON, D. R. *Corporate Culture and Organizational Effectiveness.* John Wiley & Sons, New York, NY, 1990.

[10] FALSEY, T. *Corporate Philosophies and Mission Statements.* Greenwood Publishing Company, Westport, CT, 1989.

[11] FOSTER, T. R. *101 Great Mission Statements.* Kogan Page Limited, London, England, 1995.

[12] GAST, W. F. *Principles of Business Management.* St. Louis University, St. Louis, MO, 1953. unpublished course notes.

[13] HARMON, W. W. *Global Mind Change: The Promise of the Last Years of the Twentieth Century, 1988.* Knowledge Systems Institute, Skokie, IL, 1988.

[14] HASCHAK, P. G. *Corporate Statements: The Official Missions, Goals, Principles and Philosophies of Over 900 Companies.* McFarland & Company, Jefferson, NC, 1998.

[15] JONES, L. B. *The Path.* Hyperion, New York, NY, 1996.

[16] JONES, P., AND KAHANER, L. *Say It and Live It: The 50 Corporate Mission Statements That Hit The Mark.* Currency Doubleday, New York, NY, 1995.

[17] KANTER, R. M. *Change Masters.* Simon & Schuster, New York, NY, 1983.

[18] KOBAYASHE, S. *Creative Management.* American Management Association, Inc., New York, NY, 1971.

[19] KOCH, R., AND CAMPBELL, A. *Wake Up and Shake up Your Company.* Trans-Atlantic Publications, Inc., Philadelphia, PA, 1993.

[20] LEVERING, R. *A great place to work.* Random House, Toronto, Canada, 1988.

[21] MCCOY, C. S. *Management of Values.* Pitman Publishing Inc., Marshfield, MA, 1985.

[22] MCDERMOT, D. R., URBAN, D. J., AND O'HALLARON, R. D. Developing and managing a mission statement: A study of marketing departments. *Journal of Marketing Education 18*, 1 (Spring 1996).

[23] PALUBIAK, R. C. *Corporate Mission: Think Mission Before Commission.* Business Persons Hand Book Volume 4. Optima Consulting Group, St. Louis, MO, 1998.

[24] PETERSEN, D. E., AND HILLKIRT, J. *A Better Idea.* Houghton Mifflin Company, Boston, MA, 1991.

[25] Speed of Ford's comeback surprised even the CEO. St. Louis Post Dispatch, Sunday, October 22, Page 12E, Business Section 1989.

[26] REED, S., DAWLEY, H., AND ROSANT, J. British Airways sure isn't coasting. *Business Week* (September 30 1996), 52.

[27] SATHE, V. Implications of corporate culture: A manager's guide to action,. *Organizational Dynamics, Periodical Division of the American Management Association, 1601 Broadway, New York, N.Y.* (Autumn 1983).

[28] SCOTT, C., TOBR, G., AND JAFFE, D. *Organizational Vision Values and Mission.* Crisp Publications, Menlo Park, CA, 1993.

[29] WALTON, M. *The Deming Management Method.* Perigee Books, New York, NY, 1986.